WITHDRAWN
from
EASTERN FLORIDA STATE COLLEGE LIBRARIES

D1570708

The Hidden Economy

THE CONTEXT AND CONTROL
OF BORDERLINE CRIME

Stuart Henry

Martin Robertson

© Stuart Henry 1978

All rights reserved. No part of this publication may be reproduced, stored in a retrieval system, or transmitted in any form or by any means, electronic, mechanical, photocopying, recording or otherwise without the prior written permission of the copyright holder.

First published in 1978 by Martin Robertson & Company Ltd., 17 Quick Street, London N1 8HL.

ISBN   0-85520-240-8

Printed in Great Britain by
Richard Clay (The Chaucer Press) Ltd,
Bungay, Suffolk

Contents

The members of the jury were requested to complete claim forms for expenses they had incurred while fulfilling this civic duty. On filling these in, there was considerable discussion concerning which items could be inflated, such as mileage by car, and whether to risk the claim that by fulfilling their jury service they had lost their normal weekly wage. After payment had been made, there were comparative calculations on the amount of money that had been illegally obtained, or 'spending money' as one of them called it. The money acquired in this fashion ranged from £3 to £25. No one condemned this practice or reported it to policemen on duty at the court; yet, shortly before, the same men had found an adolescent guilty of stealing items valued at 50 shillings, and had all morally condemned his behaviour by agreeing with the judge's sentence of nine months in prison.

Steven Box (1971:63)

ACKNOWLEDGEMENTS

Some of the material in this book has been used in my previously published pieces and is reproduced here with kind permission of the respective journals: 'It fell off the back of a lorry', *New Society* (26 February 1976), pp. 427–9; 'Fencing with Accounts: The Language of Moral Bridging', *The British Journal of Law and Society*, Vol. 3 (1976), pp. 91–100; 'The Other Side of the Fence', *The Sociological Review*, Vol. 24 (1976), pp. 793–806; and 'On the Fence', *The British Journal of Law and Society*, Vol. 4 (1977), pp. 124–33. Parts of Chapter 6 are to appear in an article written with Gerald Mars entitled 'Crime at Work: The Social Construction of Amateur Property Crime', to be published in *Sociology* in 1978.

Preface

This book is about the property crimes committed by ordinary people in legitimate jobs. It is about the pilfering and fiddling of goods and services that goes on every day in factories, shops and offices up and down the country. It describes the context in which these crimes occur, the relationships between the people who take part in them and the sub-economy that they form. It looks beyond technical property theft into a world where the acquisition and exchange of 'cheap' goods, 'bent gear' and 'bits and pieces' have a personal flavour; where the buying and selling of stolen goods signifies doing favours for workmates, friends and relatives. It describes how the relationships among 'trading partners' and the flow of goods between them forms a hidden economy within our society. *my essay is*

At a broader level, the book is fundamentally concerned with how we see the property crimes of others and how we fail to see the same crimes in ourselves. It focuses on how our ambiguous way of talking lets us see fiddling as something everyone else does and as an activity which ought to be stopped. But at the same time it shows how we object to the least curtailment of our own perks. Importantly, then, *The Hidden Economy* is about our conflicting sense of honesty and dishonesty. It is essential that we understand the nature of this conflict if we are to transcend our present crime-control cul-de-sac–the position where the only solution to the 'growing crime problem' is more 'law and order'. I believe that only by probing the *context* of crime will it ever be understood. Only by *acknowledging* its context will we be able to formulate appropriate policies for its control or assimilation into our society.

The book does not use the hidden economy as a phenomenon through which various theories of crime and society may be tested. It does not, for example, explicitly develop the idea that social order is maintained by minimising ambiguity and by dealing only in discrete categories of behaviour which are morally rated as good or bad; honest or dishonest. Instead, my aim has been to report what actually goes on among people who engage in the hidden economy and to describe the various methods which have been used to control it. For this reason the book is intended for anyone who is involved in the crime control business and everyone who is interested in how near they are to the borderline of crime.

In relation to this book there are many people whose help I gratefully acknowledge. I am most thankful to Gerald Mars who, during many meetings including walks in the pouring rain on Hampstead Heath, gave an incredible stimulus to my thinking and provided the anthropological dimension of the book. It was he who first coined the phrase 'The Hidden Economy' and he who has done more than anyone to get it seriously researched and debated. Steven Box must be credited with the original idea to study 'the secondary economic system of stolen goods' and for supervising the research for my Ph.D. thesis, during which time he fostered in me a spirit of self-reliance. The research itself was supported by a Social Science Research Council grant and was carried out at the University of Kent at Canterbury. Since 1976 I have received considerable benefits from meeting fellow members of the Outer Circle Policy Unit's working party on 'The Hidden Economy'.

The greatest aid came from all those 'ordinary people' who so generously told me about their own fiddles, dodges and deals and who, despite the legacy of Richard Milhous Nixon, allowed me to tape-record our interviews. But considerable assistance also came from colleagues in the field. Jason Ditton's early critical comments have helped greatly and he has provided much in the way of competitive stimulus. Forthright criticism and comment came from Carl Klockars, Ted Ferdinand, John Tobias and John Mack. Mr D. A. King of the Kent Probation and After-Care Service, Christine Fox, May Hobbs and Michael

Phillipson all gave me help in obtaining material and early advice on how best to tackle the research. More recently, Stan Cohen, James Cornford and Paul Rock have encouraged me with their enthusiastic interest. At a practical level I am extremely grateful to Angie Boorman and Gill Petters who typed the Ph.D. thesis, and Pat Davis who typed the manuscript for this book. Criticism of style and argument has been painstakingly provided by Ruby Bendall whose outstanding ability to highlight grammatical slips, weak links and poor argument has been an invaluable help to me. Most of all, I am indebted to Sally Henry who has sustained the whole project with her constant support and encouragement, critical comment, editorial advice and, most especially, her wisdom in never accepting a word I say.

Stuart Henry
30 September 1977

Addiction Research Unit
Institute of Psychiatry
University of London

1. Introduction: Hidden Crime and the Hidden Economy

> The investigation of unregistered criminality will, even if it does not bring about any revolution in general outlook on crime and criminals, certainly challenge some of the established dogmas of present day criminology.
>
> *I. Anttila* (1964:414)

In 1964 the founder of the Cambridge Institute of Criminology estimated that, however high the official crime figures might be, no more than 15 per cent of all crimes committed are ever brought into the open, leaving 85 per cent of crimes hidden or unaccounted for (Radzinowicz, 1964). Since then, many different people, including journalists, criminologists, sociologists, academics, laymen, police and security officers, have speculated upon the nature and causes of the 'dark figure' of hidden crime. Most have attempted to account for the omissions by suggesting that they occur when crimes are inaccurately reported, subject to biased recording, or simply undiscovered.

Often crimes do not get reported because there are no particular victims to become indignant, grieved or distressed. Many unreported crimes are public property offences and, unlike 'normal' property crimes such as theft, burglary and robbery, involve no specific victim to report the loss. For example, no one person suffers as a result of offences such as tax evasion, welfare and social security 'scrounging', corporate fiddles and business crimes, and as a result the police rarely learn of these offences. Dennis Chapman has cited a number of such property crimes in a list of offences that he says are rarely subject to interference

1

from the police. These include false tax returns, customs offences, sales tax offences, offences related to agricultural subsidies, bribery practices by manufacturers and wholesalers to gain favours from large buyers, offences against the Factory Acts, offences against the Food and Drug Acts and conspiracies by antique dealers at auction sales to eliminate competition (Chapman, 1968:87).

There is, in addition, a variety of property crimes in which the victims may not realise they have lost anything. Steven Box points out that company owners and managers, for example, often remain ignorant of embezzlement and other commercial frauds, and store owners remain unaware of shoplifting or employee theft, particularly where stock shrinkage could just as easily result from poor accounting procedures or recording practices (Box, 1971:62). But even when they do learn about the offences, victims of such crimes are often unlikely to report them to the authorities. In England, for example, it has been shown that employee theft is reported to the police in only one in four cases (Martin, 1962:90) while in America employees are prosecuted on only one-fifth of the occasions when the offence has been found out (Robin, 1970:121). The same pattern of non-reporting occurs for particular hidden property offences such as shoplifting (Sellin, 1937; Cameron, 1964; Home Office, 1973) or tax evasion and avoidance (Sandford, 1977; Field, 1976).

Not only do hidden property crimes go unreported and therefore unrecorded, but they also fail to show up in the theft loss totals. Exactly ten years after Radzinowicz made his revelatory statement about 'hidden crime', *Security Gazette*, in its Twelfth Annual Theft Loss Survey, estimated the grand total of officially recorded theft in Britain to be £100 million. But it pointed out that its estimate did not include

> fraud, forgery, embezzlement and kindred offences, nor unreported theft, 'fiddling' and the taking of unofficial 'perks' by employees in factories, shops and offices. Nor do they include the great bulk of shoplifting offences ... The *Security Gazette* totals, therefore, only represent the 'tip of the iceberg' where the total losses due to crime are concerned. (*Security Gazette*, 1975:378)

The 'discovery' of hidden property crimes, then, has provided a feast of unstudied material for academics and students of crime. Surprisingly, though, it is only since 1970 that interest has really begun to escalate. With the exception of an early study by J. P. Martin (1962) on employee theft and the few studies that have looked at specific crimes such as embezzlement (Cressey, 1953), shoplifting (Cameron, 1964), receiving stolen goods (Henry, 1976) and computer fraud (Ditton, 1977a), most of the research work has been concerned with investigating the hidden property crimes that occur in particular occupations. Three groups of employees that have received much attention in this connection are workers in the service industries, such as hotel and catering staff (Mars, 1973; Mars and Mitchell, 1976), bread salesmen (Ditton, 1977c) and milkmen (Bigus, 1972); shopworkers (Robin, 1965; Franklin, 1975; England, 1973; 1976); and factory workers (Horning, 1970). Dockers have traditionally been associated with hidden property crimes (Mars, 1974) but studies have not been restricted just to 'working-class' occupations. They include the part-time crimes of such 'middle-class' professionals as pharmacists (Quinney, 1963) and lawyers (Richstein, 1965).

It is not only academics and researchers who have become aware of the existence, extent and importance of hidden property crime. The national press have been close behind, choosing the more common phrase 'on the fiddle' to highlight employee and other hidden property crime.

According to reports in our national news media, everyone is now 'on the fiddle'. We are told that there are very few people who are able to claim that they have never obtained goods, money, services or other benefits in unorthodox ways which, if probed deeply, would reveal that an illegal infringement, if not a crime, had been committed. Thus, in a two-page *Sunday Mirror* spread called 'Britain on the Fiddle', James Pettigrew explained that 'as money gets tighter and harder to come by in Britain, more and more people are finding new ways to make ends meet. And that, for millions, means going on the fiddle' (Pettigrew, 1977:22). He described how ticket collectors, barmen, waiters, window cleaners, shop staff, publicans, garagemen, builders, businessmen and bosses, as well as shoppers,

3

drivers, passengers, doctors and office workers are ripping off 1.8 per cent of the country's annual £73,000 million output.

Other newspapers have offered similar stories. On the front page of the *Daily Express*, Philip Aris described '£1 billion that fell off a lorry', saying that everyone is fiddling, and that 'it's considered one of the "perks" of the job, accepted by managements to make up for low wages' (Aris, 1976:1). In the *Daily Mirror*, fiddling was heralded as 'the great British rip-off' (Price, 1977:26), and consumers were warned of the many different ways they might be 'cheated'. *The Guardian* and *The Sunday Times* handled more specific reports on fiddling in the bread industry with fun titles like 'Fiddling with no strings' (Parkin, 1976:13), and 'How bread salesmen sneak their slice of the profits' (May, 1977:3). Similarly, the *Sunday Times* reported hotel and restaurant catering rackets under the title 'Fiddling while the roast burns' (Fryer, 1976:45).

In a front page exposé screaming 'Stop Thief!', *The Sun* proclaimed that people were now on the fiddle 'to the tune of a billion' (Kay, 1976:1), and its editorial comment indicted the British for being a nation of petty thieves: 'Who can put hand on heart and swear: I never did the firm out of a halfpenny? The truth is that we are ALL at it.' The answer was endorsed by a B.B.C. *Man Alive Programme* on fiddling, in which only one member of a twelve-person 'jury' was prepared to swear that she had never, ever, fiddled (Wallis, 1976).

Fiddling is the common term applied to the variety of part-time property crimes which have been known separately as: pilfering, pinching, poaching, purloining, filching, finagling, flanking, dodging, diddling, dealing, stealing, smuggling, sneaking, gouging, scrounging and screwing. Many of these activities are also known as perks, legitimate fringe benefits or entitlements that are 'allowed' to workers as a result of their being employed in a particular kind of job. A number of specific fiddles make up hidden property crime. These include acts ranging from taking company stock home from work to doing jobs 'on the side'. In the motor industry, for example, car workers have been known to take home enough component parts from their factory to assemble complete motor vehicles. Similarly, council workmen have been found to overestimate for building jobs

4

and to use the 'extra' for their own private building projects. Office workers are renowned for 'collecting' pens and stationery. 'Overloads' and 'burst' loads are common 'pickings' in the transport industry and dockers and baggage loaders syphon off a proportion of the traffic that they handle.

Personal use of the firm's telephone, photocopying or mailing service accounts for a certain amount of the kind of fiddling which may be claimed as perks, and overestimates of petrol, food and travel allowances that appear as inflated expense accounts might also be seen in this way. In addition, there are a number of other activities which feature prominently in a discussion of fiddles, such as short-changing, overloading, overestimating, under-the-counter selling, buying off-the-back-of-a lorry goods, fiddling time, dodging fares and smuggling duty-free goods. Nor should we neglect the numerous tax and social security fiddles involving undeclared income, falsely claimed allowances and misrepresented welfare benefits and rebate claims; nor corporate fiddles, such as computer fraud and industrial bribery.

Taken together, these property crimes are a significant feature of modern life, comprising a *hidden economy* operating within the legitimate economy of society. Indeed, this is the way they have been described by the recently established Outer Circle Policy Unit that has gathered together criminologists, sociologists, anthropologists, accountants, lawyers, trade union specialists, tax experts, students of welfare benefits and politicians to look into the whole area. Jason Ditton, one of the Unit's members, has described the 'hidden economy' in the following way:

These practices taken together produce what we may here refer to as a 'hidden economy.' Merchandise is regularly and 'invisibly' stolen, covered, transported, exchanged, purchased and consumed in ways that never 'come to light'. The 'hidden economy' may be defined as the: 'Sub-commercial movement of materials and finance, together with systematic concealment of that process, for illegal gain'. The hidden economy is a microcosmic, wry reflection of the visible economic structure, upon which it parasitically feeds ... The 'hidden economy', then, runs to the 'side' of the legitimate ... and

5

occasionally *all* invisible earnings are referred to as 'side money'. (Ditton, 1976a:275)

As I hope to demonstrate during the course of this book, there is much more to the hidden economy than the pursuit of gain. Indeed, it is arguable whether the hidden economy 'parasitically feeds' off the legitimate economy. However, for anyone looking at the historical evidence, it would be difficult to arrive at any other view.

DEALING IN THE PAST

In spite of the considerable attention it has been given in the last two years, the hidden economy is not new. Its history can be traced back to the thirteenth century, when it appears to have been much the same as it is today. According to Jerome Hall, fiddles of 'office' are probably the oldest property crimes in history. Aristotle spoke of the embezzlement of funds by road commissioners and other officials, and in thirteenth-century England, the Articles of Edward I provided for the investigation of 'overseers of works' who, by adjusting the accounts, acquired 'stone or timber which should have gone into public construction' (Hall, 1952:36). The *Mirror of Justice* expands on similar offences of the time, which it calls 'perjury against the King'. Such perjury would be committed by 'those who receive more from their bailiwick than they answer for to the King' (Whittaker, 1895:19). The same document also speaks of 'baliffs, receivers, and administrators of other persons' goods who steal in rendering account'. These offences can be seen as direct forerunners of tax dodging, evasion or avoidance.

Men in holy orders also took part in criminal activity. Indeed, in the twelfth century Abbot Samson of Bury was famed for fiddling the Lord of the Manor, Adam de Cuckfield, out of his best timber by marking trees that were designated to be cut down in such a way that he kept the best timber for himself. Earlier in his clerical career the Abbot had melted down all the church silver and replaced it with plated ornaments.

6

According to John Bellamy, in his study *Crime and Public Order in the Later Middle Ages*, many other people of high office, rank and status helped or participated in some illegal activity while engaged in their legitimate jobs. He says this was because 'an official position did not guarantee either good pay or regular pay, whereas the information it provided could be turned into a definite profit' (Bellamy, 1973:68).

The activity of fiddling accounts 'by the highest officials' was considerable in the fourteenth century, observed Luke Pike in his *History of Crime in England* (1873:261). By 1589, Queen Elizabeth I had a statute directed against 'persons who embezzled munitions of war which had been entrusted to them' (Act 31 Eliz. c.4) and a statute of James I's made it criminal for any person in the wool industry to 'imbezil any Wool or Yarn delivered to him to be wrought' (Act 7 Jac. I.7).

Pilfering by people in honest jobs was also prevalent and was known as 'Larceny by Servant'. Hall says that this was recognised as a problem as early as 1339, but was disregarded in the 1344–5 Statutes of Edward III (Hall, 1952:7). However, in 1529 Henry VIII had made it a felony for a servant to take his master's goods (Act 21 Hen. VIII c.7). More descriptively, the second part of John Awdeley's *Fraternity of Vagabonds*, written in 1561, was entitled 'A Quartern of Knaves' and contained an elaborate catalogue of the different types of 'bad' servants. Whether or not it owes more to imagination than observation, as some have suggested (Salgãdo, 1972:15), it nevertheless shows that by 1561 'employee' pilfering, stealing, dealing and even fiddling time were familiar patterns of behaviour. Among his twenty-five orders of knaves he included:

7. Rinse Pitcher ... is he that will drink out his thrift at the ale or wine and be oft-times drunk. This is a licorish [greedy] knave that will swill his master's drink and bribe [take dishonestly] his meat that is kept for him ... 16. Munch-Present ... is he that is a great gentleman, for when his master sendeth him with a present, he will take a taste thereof by the way. This is a bold knave, that sometime will eat the best and leave the worst for his master ... 19. Dyng Thrift ... is he that will make his master's horse eat pies

and ribs of beef and drink ale and wine. Such false knaves oft-times will sell their master's meat to their own profit ... 24. Nunquam [never] ... is he that when his master sendeth him on an errand he will not come again of an hour or two where he might have done it in half an hour or less. This knave will go about his own errand or pastime and saith he cannot speed at the first. (Awdeley, 1575:74)

In the same period, keepers of pubs, brothels and lodging houses were noted to be doing a certain amount of illegal trading besides their legitimate business. In 1592 Robert Greene, in a tract on 'Cony-Catching', wrote about '... special receivers of stolen goods, which are of two sundry parties: either some notorious bawds, in whose houses they lie ... or else they be brokers, a kind of idle sort of lewd livers, as pernicious as the lift [thief]' (Greene, 1592:171). A few years later, Thomas Dekker described pub owners as the main kind of 'broker' and declared that 'tippling houses called bousing kens or stalling kens, houses where they have ready money for any stolen goods ... are the nurseries of rogues and thieves' (Dekker, 1612:366). The extent to which pubs and lodging houses were merely 'covers' for criminal enterprises, as the contemporary writers would lead us to believe, is difficult to assess. But it is unrealistic to suppose that there were not many people whose activity lay somewhere between the criminal receiver and the legitimate businessman; that is, they ran primarily legitimate businesses but were also doing some illegal trading on the side.

Patrick Colquhoun provides us with one of the few elaborate examples of part-time fiddling, dealing and stealing as a hidden economy among people working in the Port of London at the end of the eighteenth century. He describes how watchmen took a 'small gratuity' of half a crown to take no notice of smuggling transactions. He tells of mariners plundering cargo in storage, placing it where it was easy to get at so that it could be picked up by friends and taken to 'the house of a receiver'. Especially illustrative is the following report of a network of on-the-side activity. He says the system of plunder ... was always carried on by the connivance of the Mate and Revenue Officers in consequence of a preconcerted plan, and agreement to pay them a certain sum of money, for the liberty of opening and removing from such cases and packages as were accessible, as much sugar, coffee, and other articles as could be conveyed away . . . the Mate and Revenue Officers . . . generally went to bed while the mischief was going forward, that they might not see it. These infamous proceedings were carried on according to a regular system. The gangs . . . were generally comprised of one or more Receivers, together with Coopers, Watermen, and Humpers who were all necessary in their different occupations . . . The Receivers generally furnished the money necessary to bribe the Officers and Mate in the first instance and also provided the Black Strap [bags made to carry 100 lbs of sugar and dyed black, to prevent them from being seen at night]. The Waterman procured as many boats as were wanted. The Humpers unstowed the casks in the hold. The Coopers took out the leads and all hands afterwards assisted in filling the bags . . . The dreadful system of Night Robbery was not confined to sugar alone. Whenever coffee made part of the cargo, the plunder of that . . . was enormous. Rum was also pillaged in considerable quantities . . . All the ships thus circumstanced were denominated *Game Ships*. (Colquhoun, 1800:58–61)

More recently, Bob Gilding (1971) has described how coopers also used to 'sample' the contents of the casks and barrels which they were responsible for maintaining. Drinks, which were unofficially siphoned from a wine tub or pumped from a cask using a 'jigger', were known as 'waxers'; those gained by 'sweating' the alcohol out of tubs by using boiling water were known as 'bull'. He also mentions that dockers customarily took their 'sweepings' from the employer's cargoes. George Pattison similarly describes the theft of rum and sugar which was 'an easier object to conceal and convey through the dock gates, while the fact that sugar casks were frequently found on arrival to be broken to pieces, gave sugar coopers special opportunities for plunder' (Pattison, 1850). Moreover, 'breakages', 'shortages' and suchlike were an accomplished form of fiddle used to conceal pilfering in the docks. As Colquhoun

9

recognised, 'Deficiencies which frequently were imputed to inaccuracies and mistakes in shipping the cargo were, in fact, the result of deliberate acts of villany, committed under circumstances where no clue to a discovery could be found or where the owners or ships' masters were saddled with the ultimate loss' (Colquhoun, 1800:57).

By the nineteenth century, instances of pilfering, fiddling and dealing were reported to have occurred in almost every occupation and, importantly, within legitimate jobs. John Tobias has said, for example, that among young people in Birmingham, 'the most prevalent crime was larceny from their masters or from ships, committed by youngsters who had an honest job' (Tobias, 1972:173). A further feature of Birmingham's urban trade was the high proportion of non-resident apprentices who were able to sell portions of their master's property on their way home. Likewise, Manchester was noted for being a place where the 'working population committed minor but repeated crimes' and much of this was done as a side-line by people who removed cotton and other materials from the mills or other places of work when the opportunity arose (Tobias, 1972:165).

One of the important aspects of this on-the-side trading was that, having taken the opportunity, the employee could rely on an understanding of what he was doing on the part of other tradesmen whom he could trust not to betray him. They would choose to accept his explanation at face value as it provided them with a useful justification for buying cheap goods. A classic case of such an arrangement is found in the following account of three master tailors who purchased goods 'off a young man in the employ of a draper of considerable business'.

The culprit had robbed his master of about £500 worth of goods which he had disposed among a numerous body of tailors, persons he had become acquainted with through the large trade his master carried on, and he had induced these tradesmen to become his customers, by stating to them that he was shortly going into business for himself; that he was then, by an agreement with his employer, allowed to do business for himself; and that he had money which enabled him to purchase for ready cash and sell cheap again. As he was a steady young man many were, by his representation, induced to encourage his efforts thinking they were seeing an industrious and worthy person. (anonymous, 1832:490)

EXPLAINING THE HIDDEN ECONOMY

At a superficial level, it might seem that a simple explanation of the hidden economy is all that is required. Jason Ditton, for example, has put forward a theory that hidden-economy activity used to exist as the customary right of common people and he says, 'The extended package of common rights . . . made a significant material contribution to the domestic household budgets of tenants' (Ditton, 1977b:41). He argues that the Acts of Enclosure of the eighteenth century effectively took away those rights and made them into crimes. Wood gathering, game rights and grazing, for example, became wood theft, poaching and tresspassing.

Similarly, it is not difficult to connect the apparent increase in present-day, part-time property crime with the prevailing economic climate. In a time of rapid inflation, when prices are high, money scarce, incomes restrained and taxation crippling, and when the only policy offered by governments is one of equality of sacrifice, no one is surprised that people respond by finding their own method of survival. If these methods involve a dodge here or a fiddle there, accepting a 'cheap' offer, stretching a perk or striking a bargain, can people be blamed? Faced with no alternative way of getting round the inflexibilities of a rigid official system, it seems hardly surprising that such things happen.

Closer examination, however, shows that these simple explanations are far from adequate. The evidence that unlawful fiddling and pilfering by 'servants' and 'office' holders existed prior to the eighteenth century considerably undermines the Acts of Enclosure theory as a cause of hidden property crime. Moreover, in spite of the considerable attention the hidden economy has recently received from researchers, media and government, there is no evidence of any sudden increase in either its size or its activities. Indeed, not only are all estimates of the overall size of the hidden economy extremely unreliable and those of any part of it imprecise, but also no measurements, computations or estimates have previously been made. There are, therefore, no comparative measures of the hidden economy, so we cannot determine whether it has changed in any way.

However, the current increased attention in the activities of the hidden economy *can* be explained by the current economic situation. When times get hard and money gets tight, people become pressured to find new ways of saving and of making sacrifices. At a time of relative economic hardship not only do we look to the wind, sea and sun for new sources of energy and new ways to make our daily bread; the focus of public attention is also brought to bear on 'wastage', 'loss' and 'shrinkage'.

The matter of explaining the hidden economy is further complicated by the historical treatment of this kind of illegal activity. Until the last few years, no one had been prepared to see hidden-economy activities as phenomena in their own right. The belief was widely held that people were either completely honest or completely dishonest and anyone who persistently, even if only occasionally, committed an illegal offence, was dishonest. As a consequence of this assumption, no attempt was made to conduct a detailed examination of part-time property crime and its wider implications. It was preferred, instead, to concentrate upon the professional criminal and his stereotypical world. But the stereotype of the property criminal is an ill-fitting explanation for hidden-economy crime. Assuming, as it does, that property crimes are committed for the pursuit of economic gain, the dishonest criminal theory cannot account for the 'part-timeness' of hidden-economy crime. Thus, while almost all the activities comprising the hidden economy involve an illegal transfer of money, goods and services, as I will show in the next chapter, they are not the province of 'criminals', but an everyday feature of ordinary people's lives. The artificial distinction between 'honest' and 'dishonest' masks the fact that the hidden economy is the on-the-side, illegal activity of 'honest' people who have conventional jobs and who would never admit to being dishonest. More importantly, the distinction fails to

12

accommodate the finding, which I elaborate in Chapter Five, that although money may be involved in the hidden economy, a multiplicity of other factors are often more significant, not least of these being the nature of the social relationship between all those taking part in hidden-economy crime. As I argue in Chapter Seven, if motives other than money are significant, controlling the hidden economy through conventional policing and deterrent policies may be ineffective. They may, in certain circumstances, actually exacerbate the situation by creating new kinds of problems.

Finally, the hidden economy is not easily explained by the recently very fashionable labelling theory of deviance (Lemert, 1967; Becker, 1963; Matza, 1969). Labelling theory argues that crime has been institutionalised as secondary deviation by the creation of criminal identities as products of our over-reactive methods of controlling relatively insignificant rule-breaking (primary deviation). But, as we shall see in Chapter Seven, members of the hidden economy are rarely caught breaking the law, and even when they are, they are rarely sent through the criminal processing mill. Few, therefore, are labelled as criminals. However, this weak social reaction to crime does not stop the hidden economy from becoming institutionalised as a form of illegal behaviour. Indeed, it is possible, as I try to show in Chapters Three and Four, that, by preserving the relative moral honesty of people through a combination of weak social reaction and strong criminal stereotypes, hidden-economy crime can be institutionalised in what Ditton has called 'ultimate deviance' (Ditton, 1977c:180–3).

Although explaining the hidden economy may prove more difficult than we might at first have imagined, some explanation is necessary because of the economy's importance to the society in which we live. Clearly, it can be seen that the hidden economy has major implications for a number of areas of our lives; for crime, deviance, industrial relations, work incentives, industrial organisation, law, security, policing and, perhaps most important of all, our sense of moral justice. A serious examination of the whole hidden economy is long overdue. But this is not an easy task.

Unlike many areas of social life, the hidden economy is

not one which readily lends itself to research. There are no registered addresses to which letters can be sent, no information offices, secretaries or treasurers who are prepared to take the time to sit down and explain the ins and outs of what goes on. More seriously, there are no particular places where people can be found regularly doing their fiddling, dealing and stealing. For what some may argue are obvious reasons, the hidden economy is everywhere and nowhere, all about us but nowhere to be seen.

Neither is the hidden economy a single institution or phenomenon. It goes on in different forms in a variety of places. It is done by many different people for whom it is only a part, albeit an integral part, of their lives. Often people are involved in a number of separate activities which may form part of a flow of relationships. Classically, for example, an exchange network may be set up between a storeman and a driver. The storeman fiddles his stock records to produce an overload and the driver takes the overload and delivers it to a shopkeeper or a friend who, in turn, sells it to his best friend as a 'bargain'. This kind of network can be so extensive that twenty or thirty people at a time may be involved.

In this book I have focused on one area of the hidden economy, that of the on-the-side buying and selling of stolen goods. In part this narrowing was necessary in order to be able to go, in sufficient depth, into the economy's nature, structure and operation. More importantly, however, I believe the networks typical of amateur trading are central to the activities of the rest of the hidden economy. I have examined its structure, history, moral and social organisation, the rewards accruing to those who participate and its characteristics as distinct from those of the legitimate economy. In a review of its past and current regulation, I raise the question of whether we are attempting to control it in the most appropriate way, and suggest an alternative form of control for this kind of crime. My main source of material is a study of the amateur trade in stolen goods (Henry, 1976) which I undertook as a doctoral thesis. However, I also draw widely on the growing literature on the hidden economy to inform the general argument.

14

I began the study by collecting as much written material as possible on all forms of dealings in stolen goods; books, articles, reports and newspaper cuttings. At the same time, I wrote to many people who had made a special study of the subject and also to all kinds of officials who, I believed, were likely to come into contact with the amateur trade as a result of its illegal status. These included police, lawyers, security officers, trade protection societies and probation officers. I also attended local court cases whenever a person was indicted on a charge of 'handling stolen goods' (the legal term for the offence likely to have been committed).

While all of the information gained in this way was interesting, it was largely peripheral to my core interest: what goes on in everyday amateur trading. Consequently, I decided to take a job in an area of employment that I suspected had a high level of amateur trading opportunities. I later found out that the type of job is largely irrelevant to whether or not the hidden economy actually operates. All jobs contain some fiddling, stealing and dealing. This does, however, contrast with the findings of others, notably Gerald Mars (1977), who argues that some jobs, particularly those in the service sector of industry, encourage the development of 'fiddle-prone' situations.

After a few false starts, I managed to get a job as a driver/cellarman/sales assistant for a well-known wine and spirit company. This lasted for a period of two months, during which time I was able to share in the everyday fiddling, dealing and stealing which was 'part of the job'. A second job, with a stationer's, taken towards the end of the study, enabled me to confirm many of the practices which I had learned while doing the delivery job. It also highlighted many activities I had taken for granted during my time in a previous job in a photographic factory where I had worked a year earlier.

The bulk of the material for the study was obtained by way of tape-recorded interviews with twenty people whom I selected on the basis of the contrast in their jobs, their involvement in *different* trading networks and the intimacy with which

I knew them. The aim was to get as varied a sample as possible. The interviewees whose material I draw on in the text include the following: stonemason, plumber, factory manager, industrial designer, deliveryman, freelance copywriter, builder, housewife, factory worker, unemployed driver, cleaner, sales assistant, shop manager, clerical worker, lorry driver, company director and the leader of a voluntary group. Some of these people I met in the jobs I took; others I met in my previous work with the photographic processing company. The majority were people around me; neighbours, friends, relatives, university colleagues and even my local hairdresser. A small number of them were probation referrals. But the rest had never been accused, let alone indicted, for a criminal offence. In the next chapter I will show how these different characters relate to form the basic unit of the hidden economy: the trading network.

2. Trading Networks

> The subject matter is familiar: the network of friends,
> relatives and work-mates; the visiting, bargaining, gos-
> siping and manoeuvring that goes on between them
> ... the steps an ambitious man takes to build up
> his fund of credit among useful relations; and the
> operation of neighbourhood and workplace cliques
> and factions. These are the processes and situations
> with which we are all involved and they are the
> basic stuff of social life.
>
> *Jeremy Boissevain* (1974:4)

Viewed from one perspective the hidden economy is a collection
of separate activities performed by individuals working in a
variety of different shops, factories, offices and institutions. When
bread salesmen, milkmen or delivery men fiddle their customers,
when hotel staff pilfer chunks of bacon and when shop assistants
'dip the till', they are said to be working alone. The typical
shoplifter is often portrayed as a solitary operator: an Arab
tourist, a menopausal woman or a befuddled old-age pensioner.
Indeed, one researcher found that in a store he investigated
there were 150 employees separately but simultaneously stealing
(Curtis, 1960). Knowing this, it is difficult to see how some
part-time crimes could be done co-operatively. Characteristically,
hidden-economy activities, such as expense fiddles, fare dodging
and income tax evasion, are nearly always done alone, even
if the results of such activities are later shared with others.
However, many hidden-economy crimes are not done single-hand-

17

edly but in conjunction with friends, relatives and workmates who, when taken together, can be shown to form trading networks. These networks are especially likely to occur when goods are being pilfered, fiddled and subsequently sold. Take, for example, the case of shop assistants who are 'on the fiddle' with friends or relatives. When there are no store detectives about the cashier signals to a friend who is buying various goods. The cashier rings up some of the items, but lets the rest through. The extra goods obtained in this way may be shared out later between the cashier and her friend, or they may be passed on to a friend's friend for sale in a local office or factory. It is this linking of relationships through the acquisition and exchange of goods and services that forms trading networks.

Trading may take place in any kind of setting. The fact that in most workplaces some kind of unofficial dealing operates among staff is well known, but as it involves goods from outside, managements usually consider it to be relatively harmless. In the photographic firm where I worked, it was quite common for Maurice, the print-room manager, to set up a display on one of the canteen tables for the sale of his 'cheap' perfume. Likewise Lucy, an office clerk I interviewed, used to take considerable quantities of kitchen and household wares, such as Pyrex dishes, cutlery, can openers, whisks and scales, into her office for sale to 'the girls at work'. She explained: 'One of people at work might say "Can you get any more of these knives?" and one would circulate to the other and say "Can you get any more of so-and-so? Can you get any more of these spoons?" It went on like that from one to dozens to hundreds and before long it was all round the firm.'

Outside the work situation trading may take place in people's homes. For example, whenever Jim, a shoplifter, supplied cheap goods to Freddy, a plumber, there would be 'a Sunday-morning knock at the door: "I got some suits. Do you want them?"' Not surprisingly, local pubs or clubs are popular places for trading. Derek, an industrial designer, pointed out that in many pubs trading is taken for granted. 'If I was to go over the pub now and go up to the publican and say, "Is Gerry in tonight?" and look round and ask, "Has he been in?" or

"Is he going to be around?", everyone will know that I'm after something.' Derek told me that all he had to do was to ask and he could get what he wanted.

> You go in there and you're talking to someone and you say 'Do you know where I can get so-and-so?', and he'll say, 'I don't know,' but he'll shout across the bar and say, 'Pete, John,' whatever his name is, 'is your brother still getting those so-and-so's cheap?' and the word will go around both bars, and even if nobody knows, within a couple of days somebody will be found.

Sometimes the local pub may be the forum for a whole community to take part in the hidden economy, as in the case of the 'Five Bells' at Risley. For a substantial period of time, this small Bedfordshire village was the distributive centre for pilfered and fiddled goods from universities, hospitals, colleges and a transport firm. The village, with its population of 600, was described as being 'virtually awash with stolen property' (*The Guardian*, 1975:5).

In short, any place where people meet and form relationships with one another serves as an ideal context for amateur trading. For this reason I was not surprised to overhear the following conversation while travelling in a commuter train from Sidcup to London:

Man: Want a tennis dress? I might be able to get you a tennis dress.

Woman: What, from Colin's wife?

Man: No!

Woman: Oh, ask no questions?

Man: Yes, from my contact in contraband. He does badminton rackets as well. Loads of good stuff, but 'cheap'.

Woman: What size?

Man: I don't know. He says he'll bring one, well, one or two in–that's if he's got any and you can try them out.

However, the range of contexts in which hidden-economy trading takes place should not deceive us into thinking that all forms of illegal trading are of this kind. Hidden-economy trading is a special kind of illegal behaviour and is very different from other kinds of illegal trading such as fencing, black marketeering and hustling.

WHAT IS HIDDEN-ECONOMY TRADING?

In its simplest form, hidden-economy trading is the illicit buying and selling of 'cheap', usually stolen, goods that goes on among ordinary people in honest jobs. Unlike professional fencing, where the businessman-fence devotes the major part of his time and realises the vast majority of his income from his trade in stolen merchandise (Klockars, 1972; Henry, 1977), the amateur trade is done strictly as an on-the-side activity. Those who take part in the trade do not expect their illegal activities to earn them a living and, as we shall see in a later chapter, the dealer gets little personal financial profit from his activity. Ultimately, his hidden-economy enterprise is always secondary to his full-time, legitimate job. The 'part-timeness' of hidden-economy crime has been expressed clearly by Mary Cameron in discussing shoplifters:

> ... their crimes are peripheral to rather than central to their lives ... The peripheral criminal has a vocation which is legitimate. His career may be merchandising, clerical work, teaching, machine operating, nursing, truck driving, police work, medicine. His major source of livelihood is from his respectable career and he identifies with the dominant values of society.... (Cameron, 1964:184)

Buying 'cheap' or getting 'stuff that's fallen off the back of a lorry' usually means purchasing goods ranging from kitchen ware to car parts, from razor blades to television sets, at anything from a third to a half less than the price they would cost if bought from a retail shop. It means being able to get hold

20

of cheap goods, typically from factories where they are manufac-
tured, warehouses where they are stored, lorries on which they
are transported or shops where they are sold. It may involve
a variety of illicit techniques, such as shoplifting, pilfering from
work or hijacking. It may also entail the use of legal or quasi-legal
methods, such as wholesale purchasing or the sale of legal
perks, as in the case, for example, of the 'sale' of miners'
coal.

However, goods that are cheap are not *necessarily* stolen,
although it is true they are *often* obtained by illegal means.
But if stolen goods are not available, then the cheapest alternative
is found. In my study it became apparent that cheap goods
were available from a variety of sources. Steve, who had been
involved in trading networks ever since he could remember,
said:

> In our area there was a kind of rule that if you couldn't
> buy what you wanted bent, you got it trade. Whether you
> was in the trade or not, you went to great lengths to get
> it trade. And if you couldn't get it there, you got it from
> a cash-and-carry by borrowing someone's card. You never
> went into a shop and bought it. That's a mug's game.

Michael, who ran a men's hairdressing salon, boasted that
he was able to get whatever I wanted if I gave him enough
time: 'But there again,' he said, 'it's not necessarily knocked-off.
It may be straight but it'll be cheap.' He, too, pointed out
that he did not go 'out of his way' to find 'knocked-off'
goods. 'I could put you in contact with somebody who could
possibly do something for you and possibly get it straight away,
but it might be legitimate. It wouldn't necessarily be bent.'

The predominance of a market for 'cheap' goods distinguishes
hidden-economy trading from black marketeering which, in many
ways, might seem to be a similar activity. No doubt the war-time
butcher who saved cuts of meat under the counter for his
local customers operated a similar trade, as does the Russian
shop worker who puts aside scarce commodities so that her
friends do not have to queue, but, generally speaking, there
is an essential difference between black marketeering and hidden-

economy trading. Black markets only operate in an economy of scarcity, in which a rationing system and price cartels are established to ensure the even distribution of essential commodities. Should the demand become greater than the supply, the price of goods would be driven up to artificially high levels. Such a situation invites some traders to breach the price restrictions, thus creating a black market. In this market goods move illegally at prices far *above* the official price and in quantities not authorised by the rationing system (Clinard, 1952). In such circumstances individual price rises may be as much as 200 per cent. For example, an American Meat Institute survey of shops in eleven large cities, carried out just after the war, found an average overcharge of 83 per cent (anonymous, 1946:17).

In contrast to black marketeering, even when goods become difficult to obtain through legitimate trade the hidden economy still provides them at a cheaper price. As Michael said:

> This has become another racket, getting things straight away. Most of the things you go for now, you've got to wait. You know, cars, washing machines, televisions, things like this. A certain make of television. These people can get stuff straight away and they quite possibly get it far below any price you could pay for it.

But the desire consistently to supply 'cheap' goods does not mean these are of poor quality. Top-quality merchandise is the only product acceptable to the purchasers, because they are concerned to get a genuine bargain. Moreover, nothing less would be supplied by the dealer who wishes only to satisfy 'customers' in the network. Thus, rather than deal in poor-quality goods, the trader will sometimes resort to paying top prices for goods from a warehouse 'just to fill orders' (Emerson, 1971:35). All this is in marked contrast to the 'hustler', who can be found selling 'stolen' goods in a market or down Oxford Street, flashing rings or watches from under his coat or selling perfume out of a case. The hustler gives the impression that he is dealing in stolen goods. He is, in fact, a con-man who buys second-rate, inferior goods in order to sell them at a price higher than their true value. He does this by falsely claiming that the goods are stolen and relies on this to 'explain' their cheap price. So much is he conning customers that if the police stop him, he is usually able to produce a street trader's licence and a bill of sale.

WHO BUYS AND WHO SUPPLIES 'CHEAP' GOODS?

In their study of the marketing of stolen goods, Ted Roselius and Douglas Benton speculate that 'demand for stolen goods is probably relatively low in the public at large, but may be relatively high within certain low-income sectors of the population' (Roselius and Benton, 1973:182). The same assumption, that only low-income groups are attracted to stolen goods, led the President's Commission on Law Enforcement and Administration of Justice in the United States to declare that 'the redistribution of goods through theft might constitute a significant subsidy to certain groups in our society; its curtailment might have significant side-effects. . . .' (President's Commission, 1967:99).

However, as we shall see in Chapter Three, within hidden-economy trading networks goods are seldom, if ever, presented as stolen. Neither are there any elaborate efforts to disguise the illegality of the transactions. Rather, a simple but ambiguous gloss is provided and this relies on the buyer to provide his own explanation for the cheapness of the goods. The most important feature of the gloss is its reference to the goods as 'cheap' or 'bargains'. The consumer's belief that he is getting a bargain is a strong buying motive and, as the desire for bargains is virtually universal, we would expect the demand for 'cheap' goods to span all occupational, class and status groups. Thus, we should not be surprised by Carl Klockars's finding that customers seeking bargains at his fence's retail store included 'secretaries, bank tellers, executives, policemen, detectives, lawyers, tipstaffs, an occasional judge, customs officials, waterfront workers and inspectors, insurance adjusters, private detectives and crime reporters' (Klockars, 1974:104). Indeed, he points out that the largest single group of customers is connected with law enforcement. Similarly, Frank Emerson's part-time dealer, who is an electrician by trade, sells his wares to 'professionals and blue-collar workers', neighbours, policemen and a dentist'. Emerson says, 'Most of Tommy's customers, like the dentist, can afford to maintain adequate wardrobes by shopping in retail stores. But, by dealing with Tommy, they get more for less, and people are always ready for a bargain' (Emerson, 1971:34).

Of the people in my study several enjoyed a high standard of living, which they earned from their legitimate occupations. For example, Paul was a director of his own firm which sold computerised direct mail. As a majority shareholder, Paul celebrated his success by buying a new detached house, a boat, a Range Rover, a Jaguar and a Hillman. He also bought a flat in Manchester. Roy was an assistant manager with a photographic firm in Leeds. He lived with his wife and four children in a modern detached house which had an immaculately kept garden and multi-coloured tiled patio. Similarly, Stan, Michael, Steve, Dave and Derek all owned their own houses.

Some had absorbing and creative jobs which involved a strong commitment to their work. Paul ploughed his earnings back into the firm for the first year or so and, at that time, worked an eighteen-hour day. Stan was proud of his craft skills as a stonemason and often talked of going to Rome to do restoration work. Michael was a top hair stylist, while Dave's experience of converting buildings into flats was evident in his own home. In contrast, Maurice's colourful non-career included having been a clerical worker, tube tunnel digger, print room manager, and free-lance copywriter. Others had equally absorbing hobbies. Derek, whose job was in industrial design, was keenly interested in metal sculpture; Maurice had a deep and knowledgeable interest in rock culture and James Joyce; Stan was a brilliant snooker player; Michael enjoyed fast cars; Lucy had a keen interest in gardening and spent much of her spare time on her allotment; Dick ran a voluntary youth group.

It would seem, then, that people who buy 'cheap' goods come from a variety of different classes and socio-cultural backgrounds. More importantly, there is no clear-cut division between those who buy and those who sell. A person may buy something

24

one day and be selling something else on the next. As we shall see in a later chapter, only by being able to give and take are members able to maintain their place in the hidden-economy trading network. For example, whenever Steve had 'cheap' goods, usually cigarettes, he felt he had to 'give' them to people at work because whenever they got something they would sell it to him. Similarly, Steve's workmate, Freddy, bought things he did not really need just because his friend, Jim, was selling them cheap.

He's had about fifteen tape-recorders. He buys one and he sells one. Every time Jim comes round with a better model he'll buy it and flog his old one. He probably buys and keeps more stuff for himself than he knocks out in the long run. So many people in the family have got his old tape-recorders, it's not true. Take records. I mean, every time Jim shows up with a load of records, Freddy has about ten for himself. He just can't resist them. I should think he's got at least twelve suits. Simply because they're cheap, he feels he must have them. If you show him something that's allright, he'll be there.

In the trading networks, then, there is no separation between a class of 'dealers' and a class of 'customers'. All are buyers; all are sellers. There are, however, differences of emphasis in dealing and stealing, depending upon the type of job that a person has. Some occupations more readily lend themselves to the playing of dealer roles, while others are more suited to stealer roles.

The dealers

The jobs that are best for on-the-side dealing are those in which a large number of differently employed people meet separately, briefly and regularly. One such job is that of a roundsman delivering to regular customers. Derek, for instance, explained how his 'local, friendly coalman', supplied him with timber, bricks and general building materials:

He seems to be able to acquire most building stuff. But there are so many people that he comes in contact with through his job ... I mean, he's delivering coal, all day, every day, and he doesn't just deliver to miners, he delivers it to local firms and so on. There's a brick factory just a few miles away. I suspect that he knows someone that works there. There's a timber yard over at Fenton. I suspect that he knows someone there or somebody owes him a favour. He's given them coal, this sort of backhanded business.

Ray, himself a lorry driver for a concrete firm, told me of his ice-cream man 'who's pretty good and can get anything'. Jason Ditton has shown how on-the-side dealing works in the case of bread salesmen who set up deals for the sale of 'hot' bread, cakes or 'sidelines' of eggs, potatoes and even stolen radios and coats (Ditton, 1977c:111). Similarly, Bigus (1972) has documented the personalised dealing between milkmen and their customers.

Other jobs which create opportunities for dealing are those such as a sales representative, lorry driver or maintenance engineer, where the work requires periodic visits to different factories or offices. Maurice had a salesman friend who worked for a perfume manufacturer. He said that a favourite trick with 'reps' was to exchange their free samples.

Say they get given £1000's worth of free samples to distribute to their customers. They'll only let out £200's worth. The rest they'll change for something else. A lot of cigarette reps do this, but the guy I know works for one of the perfume companies. He takes his van round the back of the hotel and they do a swap with all the gear.

The job of a maintenance engineer can be especially appropriate. Freddy, for example, is a married man with three children, who owns his own house in Manchester and runs his own Toyota estate car. He works full time as a plumber contracted to industrial firms, mostly in the photographic processing trade for which much water is needed. While visiting the different firms in the north-west he meets many people. 'He's got regular contacts,' said Steve. 'It's not just one firm. He's got a lot of people and a lot of firms.' This gives him ample opportunity to distribute goods that he obtains from Jim, his shoplifter friend: 'It's now reached the stage that if anybody wants anything, a radio, tape recorder, electric drill or suit, they don't go and buy it, they wait for Freddy to come round and say, "Can you get it for me?"' Michael, the hair stylist, was able to trade in goods ranging from tins of fruit salad to car parts. 'Hairdressing's always been good in that respect,' he explained. 'Well, you're actually handling people. It's a very rare business. You know, there is nothing quite like it for that sort of thing. Nowhere else do you get a relationship in such a short time.'

However, in practice, there are certain reasons why legitimate retail stores are not ideal places for hidden-economy trading. Unless they are 'corner' shops, they are unlikely to provide the opportunity for establishing the highly personalised relationships which are essential before trading can take place. Secondly, they are ill suited to on-the-side dealing because there is a great temptation to offer the stolen goods directly to the public at a cut price, as part of normal trade, a practice which undermines the specialness of the trade. Thirdly, a retail shopkeeper who buys his stock 'cheap' will find it difficult to distinguish it from the normal stock and, without this distinction, much of the point of on-the-side trading is lost. Commenting on a Cardiff shopkeeper friend, Steve said:

'He'd sell it in the shop, sure, but most of the time it didn't go on the shelves because there was too much of it. He was doing it cut-price anyway, so what's the point? He used to push it on to his brother who worked in London at Lloyd's, and he'd go round touting it there. Because it wasn't a shop situation but a work situation, he'd sell more than Syd would sell in his shop.

In fact, the ideal job is any that allows the goods to be sold in an *abnormal* context. If the grocer had been selling bathroom' fittings, he would have been able to deal on the side without finding it necessary to go to great lengths to distinguish the goods from his normal stock. This is why the hairdresser traded successfully in car parts, and why bread salesmen prefer to deal in potatoes and eggs rather than cheap bread. Just as certain occupations are more conducive to dealing than others, so there are jobs which maximise the opportunities for people to supply trading networks with 'cheap' goods.

The stealers

It is not without significance that the most important case in legal history on which much of the law of theft was later based was the Carrier's Case of 1473. It concerned a defendant who was hired to carry bales to Southampton. Instead of fulfilling his obligation, he carried the goods to another place, broke open the bales and took the contents. He was charged and eventually found guilty of a felony, but considerable legal debate ensued as to whether a felony had been committed. It was argued that the defendant had lawful possession of the goods by virtue of being hired to deliver them and that 'what he himself has he cannot take . . . therefore it cannot be felony nor trespass' (Hall, 1952:4).

The passage of time, changes in culture and the complexities of modern technology have not greatly altered the fact that the transport industry is one of the chief sources of stolen or 'cheap' goods. Thus, Carl Klockars found that drivers were the main source of stolen goods for his fence.

Your truck drivers are basically honest family men. Many of 'em would never steal anything. But every time they'd get an overload, they'd drop it off to me. I've had some drivers bringing me stuff for ten years . . . I'd say that 75 per cent of my business came from drivers. (Klockars, 1974:61)

In my study I found that lorry drivers were one of the major suppliers of cheap goods to trading networks. Michael, the hair stylist, said that a lot of his stuff came from factories in the form of cartons which were dropped off lorries. 'We used to get loads of tins of stuff. Tins of peas, beans, fruit

28

salads, things like this. Used to get a couple of crates come in, say, once a month that had come out of a factory.'

Steve explained how the system of supply worked for his friend, whose shop was part of a grocery chain-store. The stores are independent, but each of the grocers in the chain can buy stock from large cash-and-carry warehouses. The grocers have to agree to order a certain amount of stock in advance if they are to be allowed to belong to the chain-store group. They benefit from joint advertising and discount buying. 'Well, the blokes at the warehouse would say to the lorry driver, "Bung this on your lorry and so-and-so will have it on the round." The drivers give the blokes in the warehouse ten quid each not to notice anything. A lorry driver would show up at Syd's shop with his regular order and the driver might say, "I've got a load of cheap stuff for you", which Syd had already agreed to have.'

Arranging for goods to be delivered by a driver in this way can sometimes be hazardous, because the amount delivered may be far in excess of what can easily be handled. Take, for example, the case of Paul, the company director, who began by accepting the offer of a colour television for £60.

O.K., right, but I didn't know anything about how many's coming round. When this guy knocked on the door and said to me, 'I've got it', I expected to see a small Ford Transit. Outside was a fifteen-ton lorry and when he pulled the back up, it was just crammed full of them. So I said to this chap, 'What am I s'posed to do with 'em?' and he said, 'Can you get rid of any?' So you think to yourself, allright, well, I'll do this guy a favour. He's got a load of 'em and he can't move 'em. So I spent all afternoon and evening and got rid of every one. You know, somebody else knew somebody else. So this guy went round in this big lorry all night 'cause he had to get it back, and I had to go round and collect all the money in. But even he didn't make much on it, because it had to go back to the 'goods inwards', the boys in 'the admin'. You know, he reckoned they made about a tenner each, but that wasn't bad 'cause he was taking all the risks. You know, if he got stopped with that lorry ... O.K., he had the goods received note and everything's above board, but what was he doing outside my place, you know, unloading them in the middle of the night?

Where goods are overloaded, a storeman, who is responsible for the paper work and the loading of lorries, often co-operates with the driver. Stan said that he had a friend who worked for a washing machine company, delivering machines: 'When he's loading up a consignment with the storeman, the bloke who is doing the loading says. "How many we got on today, Jo?" "Fifty washing machines." Right, on goes fifty-six. So that's six machines extra. He tells the bloke who is selling them, who gives him a back-hander, and the bloke who's loading them and carting them away also gets a share.'

The storeman is an integral part of this system, as he can place the goods on the lorry in such a way that the overload will pass unnoticed. Crucially important, however, is that he should be in a position to 'fiddle' the books, money or stock records, so that the loss is covered up. 'Like the guy who gets the car parts,' said Michael, 'he gets them straight from the factory where they are made. He goes in there and gets a few more put on. You know, he drops them a fiver, say, and gets a couple of car wings put on. Just a kind of back-hander because they can always write them off as damaged stock or something like that.' Michael pointed out that it all depended on how well you knew the guy in the stores: 'You can often get twice the quantity that you actually buy.'

Writing off stock as 'damaged', 'broken' or 'missing' is the simplest form of fiddle to cover losses. In a report on pilfering from industry, Palmer pointed out that the practice of writing off stock is often tolerated by management, who would rather turn a blind eye to the losses than upset employees with strict security checks (Palmer, 1973). In many instances, accounting systems reveal these kinds of losses in the form of 'stock shrinkage', for which a figure of between 2 and 5 per cent is considered acceptable. Storemen take full advantage of the acceptability of shrinkage, as Derek told me.

You know the electricity people, the stock they carry is

30

nobody's business. I've a friend who works there who's supplied me with bearings, free paint, sandpaper and tools, including a couple of micrometers, a torque wrench and a socket set. I mean, this is stuff he can legitimately write off as a store-keeper. The companies write so much off as waste, and these are the people who are wasting it. And everybody, I mean storekeepers all over the country, are doing it.

If storemen are shortloading rather than overloading, they need not collude with a driver on the inside, but can supply the trade directly themselves. One way in which this works is when the goods have to be stacked on a pallet ready for fork-lifting onto a lorry. A middle section of the stack is left empty and the goods that should have been there are hidden out of sight, ready to be picked up later and sold privately. This kind of operation carried on by cargo handlers is described by Frank Emerson. He says the mainstay of his amateur dealer's operation is high-quality clothing, pilfered by a freight handler who works in the cargo shed of an international carrier at Kennedy Airport: 'By checking the manifest orders on incoming cargo,' says Emerson, 'the freight handler can spot and select the merchandise he knows Tommy can use.' After selecting the two cases of freight he wants, the handler removes them from the cargo flow rack and places them with other freight near a side door. 'As far as company records are concerned,' says Emerson, 'the two cases now become "missing en route"' (Emerson, 1971:35). In this example, Tommy, the dealer, collects the cases himself by driving to the side door of the cargo shed and having them loaded into the back of his car by the handler.

Another way in which storemen, warehousemen or cargo handlers may trade without an inside driver is by co-operating with each other. Here they share the contents of the carefully acquired cases among themselves and each takes out a small quantity for sale. Mars, in his study of dockers, reports that on one occasion a crate was opened by a docker, but 'its allocation was divided among all gang sections ... My main informant, a stower, had two radios–one of which he sold'· (Mars, 1974:218). Similarly, sales assistants may be able to

31

sell directly to a dealer. This pattern is likely to occur when the seller has a legitimate sales outlet, such as a wholesaler who sells merchandise to a particular trade. An example of this typical operating pattern was reported in a recent court case. Two men working behind the counter of a builders' merchant were 'selling goods cheaply "on the side"' to self-employed builders and plumbers. The goods sold included copper joints, metal couplings and boilers, belonging to the firm. These items were sold at half price by the two sales assistants, who then split the money equally between themselves (*Kent Herald*, 1973:1).

Often the system of acquiring cheap goods is simpler and less easily recognisable as actual theft. It consists of small-scale pilferage carried on over a period of time. Michael said that all big factories were good places to get stuff from: 'Take the tile people. A lot comes out of there. I think nearly every man in there is at it. You know the plastic gutterings, you wouldn't think they could lift those, but they do. They roll them up in little tiny rolls and put them in their pockets.' Unlike the storeman–driver networks, then, simple pilferage may involve only one man. Council workmen, for example, may get extra materials that they can pass on to friends. Roy, an assistant manager in a photographic processing company, told me how he got 'cheap' paint from a friend who worked in local government. He said he used to over-order on the jobs. They would make an estimate of the amount of paint required for doors and windows for a whole street and 'what is left over local government don't want to know about, so they've got to "lose" it.' Also, 'they might estimate for two coats, but only give it one, something like that. So he puts what's over in the back of his motor and brings it round to me and I'll flog it round the works.' Numerous similar small-scale operations occur in offices and factories, and sometimes involve services rather than goods. A Post Office worker told me how he services his local resident's association with photocopying facilities: 'No one notices the odd few copies. Anyway, I don't do all of them; my wife does some.' His wife works for a bank.

While most of the goods feeding trading networks come from institutionalised fiddling and pilferage, there are other sources.

Freddy, Steve's workmate, who was a plumber, was supplied by Jim, a full-time shoplifter who specialised in stealing ready-made suits.

What he does, he reckons he can take one off the stand and sort of sweep it round like that so it's rolled up round his arm. Then it's suit on the hanger down his trousers, hanger and all, and he does his overcoat up and is out double quick. He'll show up at Freddy's place, maybe on a Sunday morning, knock at the door, 'I got some suits. Do you want them?' and he might bring round ten or fifteen and Freddy will buy five or six.

Whatever the origin of cheap goods, and however appropriate a person's occupation may be in terms of the opportunities it provides for stealing or dealing, that person will not become part of a trading network unless he first satisfies certain conditions. The real criterion governing who buys and who supplies is less a structured work role and more how inter-personal relationships are formed, conducted and developed. Acceptance in a trading network, just as for any social enterprise, depends on how a person is assessed in the eyes of the existing members.

BECOMING A MEMBER

Clearly, the removal of goods and services from legitimate trade to the hidden economy provides an overall benefit for the recipient economy. The availability of 'cheap' goods from a particular trading network also represents considerable benefits to any individual involved. In circumstances in which belonging to a group entitles a person to certain benefits it is not unusual for the group to limit its membership to particular kinds of people. This is especially so when the group's existence can be threatened by the discovery of the illegality of its activities.

Typically, hidden-economy trading will only take place among friends, relatives and workmates. Members of a trading network

33

talk of 'passing goods on' to their brothers, cousins and uncles, of dealing with the family, good friends, mates and 'the girls at work'. For example, Stan said he 'largely keeps it in the family and his friends'. He said he would not offer stuff to anyone else. Paul was quite explicit about the kind of people in his network.

You certainly wouldn't do this with a stranger. I'd only do it with people I was fairly close with. I wouldn't do it with any Tom, Dick or Harry. It's only if we've known each other a very long time and we're good buddies. We go for a drink together, and we do lots of things together. See, the chaps I know at work I know as friends. He'd have to be a friend first. I'd only pass it on to friends.

Traditionally, the way such groups and networks limit their members is by the institution of various informal vetting procedures and initiation rituals. 'Rites de passage' was a term used by Arnold Van Gennep to describe the procedures which accompany the passage of an individual from one social status to another in the course of his life, and also those which mark the passage of time. He identified three stages of rites: rites of separation from a previous status, marginal rites marking a period in which an individual is detached from one status but not yet admitted to the next, and rites of entry to a new status (Van Gennep, 1909). Rights of entry are crucial to hidden-economy trading, since strangers will only be allowed into the network when they have entered into a relationship and have been assessed as 'allright'.

Forming a relationship

A relationship with a member of an established trading network may be formed in a number of ways. Living in a particular area and doing things with neighbours, such as patronising local stores, enjoying amenities or visiting local pubs, are good ways in which to start. Michael got friendly with people who came into his salon. As he explains, 'One thing led to another and they start saying, "Can I do something for you?" ' Similarly, Steve's friend, Freddy, met another friend through their wives. Steve told me: 'Freddy's wife used to pick up the kids from school and she got friendly with this other bloke's wife and eventually she started offering Freddy's wife cheap stuff.' Derek got involved through his local pub, 'just by being there, really'. He was renovating a derelict house and at lunch-times he would go over the pub for a 'jar'. He told me how he would sit and listen to the people talking and have a chat with them: 'They're really sociable. If you sit and listen, they'll talk all night and buy you drinks and you're "in" very quickly in that sense.' He said that when you can walk up to the bar and be on first-name terms with the barman, then you know that you are 'in'. But getting accepted, as Derek illustrated, was not always a quick process. It might take up to six months: 'Although they're friendly people, they'll talk to you and you can play dominoes and they'll bring you in on their darts game, it takes a long time before they really accept you. Not until you've been accepted will they ever offer you anything.' Michael confirmed that the process of forming a relationship could take a long time and that it would run over several meetings.

It doesn't happen over just one casual meeting. Something sparks something off and you strike up a relationship and then they come out with it. But it's a slow progression. It's not something that happens instantly. It only happens over three or four meetings. They get to know you. He won't just kind of offer it to you there and then. It happens that you see him in the road and say, 'Hello', or he'll be at a set of traffic lights and the next time he comes in you say, 'Oh, I saw you last week at a set of traffic lights,' and there we are ... we're getting a relationship between two people. But you've got to have a relationship. If you don't have a relationship, everything doesn't twig.

Part of the reason why forming a relationship takes time is because it is necessary to know as much as possible about

35

a newcomer before even suggesting that he becomes part of the trading network. Only after a period of time are the other members of the network in a position to know enough about the newcomer to make the suggestion. If, for example, a person has arrived in an area to live, the bush telegraph will be able to answer some essential questions. 'They know where your letters come from and how much milk you have and who comes to see you,' said Derek. 'They know the lot.' At work the same kind of process goes on. Dave, the builder, said you could easily tell who is untrustworthy, 'like you can tell what a bloke's politics is. You can tell from what people say during the course of a day.' He added that if they say things like 'I've got no time for thieves', then they are not to be trusted. Ray, the lorry driver, could also tell who was 'allright': 'By talking to blokes in work you sort of know whether they're honest and things like that. You know the people who are allright–people like me who look criminal [laugh].'

Whether or not someone is accepted depends upon whether they are liked and how far other members of the trade feel they can be trusted. If, on the basis of the information they have gleaned during the early stages of the relationship, the person comes over as 'strange', 'odd' or 'dodgy' then nothing will happen. Derek emphasised this by saying, 'If there's any sort of doubts about you as a person and they don't like you, then nothing you can say or do will induce them to do anything.' In the same way that they are cautious of 'strangers' or 'newcomers', they are careful with people they do not like. 'If your face doesn't fit,' said Derek, 'you'll go in the pub, ask the question and get no response. They would continue playing cards and whoever you are talking to would say, 'No, I can't think of anybody.' Steve described vividly how a person in his works was labelled as 'dodgy' on the basis of his behaviour, and was subsequently excluded from future trading. He said the members of the trading network would not dream of approaching the character in question. They described him as a very upright little man, a foreman, not earning particularly good money at his sheet metalwork job. They had known the man for about four or five years and he was considered useful because he rushed work through for them. 'But it was straight.

Nothing bent about it.' Steve explained that this character 'was so honest he wouldn't dream of doing anything dishonest' and said he had been introduced to him after being told that he was 'the straightest and therefore the dodgiest character you'd ever wanna meet'. Steve explained that the foreman was a person whom they went out of their way most of the time to avoid, largely because he often said that he would have liked to have joined the police.

If anything dodgy was going on they would not let that bloke in on it. They said that, through various sorts of probings, he was deadly honest and that you don't trust someone who is honest. See, there are various sorts of attitudes and beliefs and the character that doesn't share these stands out like a sore thumb, though he's never actually tested. So somewhere his ideas just don't fit. They'd already made the decision that his attitudes were different from theirs. He was morally an upright citizen and therefore someone not to be trusted. He was strict in many ways, sticking to the book, loyal to the firm and the rules. I suppose they thought that this betrayed him and it was enough to make them think his other ideas would be different as well.

Once a person has gained a reputation for being 'honest' or 'dodgy', the onus falls on him to do something about it. This happened to Lucy, who did not know the person supplying the network and, at the same time, was judged to be honest. She eventually began trading by doing something particularly helpful and thereby demonstrating her friendship and allegiance: 'He didn't ask me to sell it. Not at first. See, I went into Elsie's house one day and saw all these things and said, "Ooh, that's nice." She said, "Yes, Harry got them for me."' But Lucy points out that she found the trading difficult to 'get in on'. She said, 'I wasn't originally accepted into the circle. I was a nobody to him. I couldn't ask outright for stuff. The only way I could get it was to offer to get rid of some for him. I asked him. I thought by doing him a favour he was doing me a favour.'

Once the members of a trading network have decided that a person is 'allright' and that he shares the same attitudes to life as themselves, they may test him out with an offer or request for 'cheap' goods. Ditton observes that this often takes the form of a particularly loaded question which he describes as the 'alerting phrase'. 'Classically between sales and bakery staff the "alerting phrase" for those "in the know" is the demand for, or offer of, "extra bread".' He notes that this appears in the form of a question; 'Is there any bread about?' (Ditton, 1977c:107). Similarly, I found that trading began with what members described either as a 'test line' or a 'probe line', requesting or offering 'cheap goods', 'cheap gear' or 'cheap stuff'. Steve said, 'In our works there's a standard line that they try people out with. They say, "Would *you* like to sell me this? Not the firm, but *you*?" If the bloke doesn't twig, he's a berk. If he doesn't see it, it's forgotten and they don't push it any further. It's there in every situation. You can probe and if the bloke's with you, you're away.' Dave pointed out that people never come right out with it: 'They say, "I've got something a bit cheap here." They never say, "I've got a stolen bit of gear here." All people say is ... most people say, "I've got a cheap bit of stuff here. Want to have a go at it?" And then there's a conversation and one might say, "It's a bit the other way." And the other says, "Who's worried?"'

Usually, the offer or request for cheap goods comes up during a conversation in which one person prepares the other for the offer or request that is shortly to follow. In the case in which someone wishes to buy something, he may talk about some difficulty he has in purchasing particular items. The member of the trading network then probes a little further for details, usually in an off-hand, though interested, way. If the response is right he may offer to 'get hold of' the goods required. Michael described how such a conversation might go.

You could be talking about cars and you say, 'Ah, I just dinged me car up,' and he'll say, 'Well, what kind of car is it?' And this is the way you carry on. That's what happened in this case. He just said he wanted some wings. He was going to go and buy them down at Auto Spares and I said, 'Well, I can get them for you,' and he asked, 'how much?' and I said, 'I'll find out.'

In the case in which the member of the trading network has goods to sell, he might chat about the 'newcomer's' general need for a particular type of good. Tom, the assistant manager of a wine and spirits shop, had the following conversation with me:

Tom: Do you smoke? You don't smoke, do you?
S.H. Well, yes, I do. I don't smoke cigarettes, but I enjoy these small cigars.
Tom: Which do you like, Benson and Hedges or Manikin?
S.H. Well, I like Manikin, but are you . . . ?
Tom: Here, stick these in your pocket.

There are at least four reasons why this ambiguous form of initiation is used. In the first place, it allows those in the trade to fill in the meaning of 'cheap' goods in a way which protects them from the disturbing knowledge of the illegality of the transaction. It also provides a verbal escape route should those involved be overheard, questioned or 'misunderstood' by informers or security personnel. In addition, it protects the members of the network from being 'caught' by a hustler who explicitly proclaims his goods are stolen when they are really poor-quality products. Finally, and importantly, it reserves the right of members of the trading network to suspend or delay commitment, should the newcomer's response be inappropriate.

Indeed, even when the provisional assessment of a newcomer has been favourable, his failure to acknowledge the 'test line' or his rejection of the offer, can have a dramatic effect on the original judgement. Steve said that there was a strong unspoken understanding that everyone was willing to buy stuff cheap, and the people who turned it down became outsiders: 'The bloke who turns down cheap stuff and the bloke that never buys anything gets a reputation. There must be something odd about him. Don't mention it to him. Keep it quiet from him'. He cited the case of one man at the firm.

This bloke worked every hour of overtime he was given. He was even known to collect up empty lemonade bottles and take them back to the sweet shop at lunch-time. But he never bought a thing. Now there's a bloke that doesn't fit. Economically he's after everything he can get his hands on, but when a 'bargain' comes up, he won't buy. So he's either so tight that he won't even buy a bargain or he's dodgy. He's honest, and that makes him an outsider in their terms.

In close, integrated work units, a person's persistent rejection of an offer or request for cheap goods might result in his rejection from the working unit as well as from the trading network. In such cases, it might be necessary for him to perform an act demonstrating allegiance in order to be accepted as one of the crew. For example, in his study of stock pilferage Gerald Mars found just such a process in operation. When talking of the induction of new gang members to the dock crew, one of his interviewees recounted the case of a Salvationist. 'Because he refused to take cargo, men were suspicious and reluctant to confirm him to membership.' At the time of police enquiries on the theft of valuable wrist-watches, they 'grilled' the new member over a period of three months to get him to inform on the other dockers. 'All that time he didn't give anything away', said Mars's informant, 'He was really firm in the gang after that' (Mars, 1974:223).

Acknowledgement that the deal is on can come via movements of the eyes, gestures and other expressive signs which are typical of a 'we rationale'. That is, they are confirmation that all involved recognise that they are doing something together (Goffman, 1961:18). Whatever way it comes, mutual acknowledgement of the offer or request for 'cheap' goods marks the end of the process of becoming a member and the beginning of a series of transactions that are trading proper. Only when trading begins can a person feel that he is part of a trading network. However, before trading begins there is an additional

40

obstacle facing potential members. Since they are ordinary people in legitimate jobs, they usually have a moral inhibition against doing anything dishonest or illegal. If they are to take part in hidden-economy activities, they must be satisfied that what they do is not 'wrong'. In the next chapter, I show how a number of attitudes and ways of thinking and of talking are often unwittingly brought into play and that these render hidden-economy activities morally acceptable to the participants.

3. Honest Dishonesty

> Norms may be violated without surrendering allegiance
> to them. The directives to action implicit in norms
> may be avoided intermittently rather than frontally
> assaulted. They may be evaded rather than radically
> rejected. Norms, especially legal norms, may be neutra-
> lised. Criminal law is especially susceptible of neutrali-
> sation because the conditions of applicability, and
> thus inapplicability, are explicit stated ... The crimi-
> nal law, more so than any comparable system of
> norms, acknowledges and states the principled grounds
> under which an actor may claim exemption. The law
> contains the seeds of its own neutralisation.
>
> *David Matza* (1964:60)

In their participation in any aspect of the hidden economy
people are likely to be breaking rules. Sometimes they are
not fully aware of the rules or that they are breaking them.
Frequently, people involved in the hidden economy have an
ambivalent attitude towards specific rules. They agree that the
overall principle should be adhered to but, for various reasons,
see themselves as exceptions, or believe that in particular circumstances the rule is either inapplicable or inappropriate. Often,
rules that are broken are not laws but broad social guidelines
or local customs, and it is difficult to know whether they are
being systematically, knowingly or unwittingly broken. On many
occasions, however, the hidden economy involves breaches of
criminal law.

Regardless of its occasional or part-time characteristics, on-the-side trading in stolen goods is an aspect of the hidden economy which involves flirtation with, and often violation of, the criminal law. Under current English theft law, the purchase or sale of stolen goods is a criminal offence, offenders being liable to anything up to a maximum of fourteen years' imprisonment. The 1968 Theft Act states that:

A person handles stolen goods if (otherwise than in the course of the stealing) knowing or believing them to be stolen goods he dishonestly receives the goods, or dishonestly undertakes or assists in their retention, removal, disposal or realisation by or for the benefit of another person, or if he arranges to do so. (*Theft Act*, 1968:s22)

In spite of this law, many otherwise law-abiding people buy and sell stolen goods. Crucially important to their participation in trading activities is whether they can excuse, justify, rationalise or otherwise preserve their moral character, should their activities be subsequently questioned. Equally important is whether they know or believe the goods in which they trade to be stolen. It is the preservation of moral rectitude and the management of implicit unacceptable knowledge which makes it possible for people to be ambivalent to the law. In this chapter I shall look at each of these issues in turn.

RATIONALISING CRIME

It must be made clear that not everyone who takes part in the part-time trade in stolen goods, or in the hidden economy as a whole, subscribes either to the law or to conventional morality. In some cases the activity is seen as part of a life in which breaking the law is a daily occurrence. For example, Stan, the stonemason, told me that the people he knew were from one particular area of London:

They don't consider nickin' something wrong. It's like if I

go into work. I've got a fireplace to do next weekend. I want eighty-odd foot of stone. I don't think about whether I'll get done or not. All I think is I want eighty foot of stone and I've got a buyer for it. If the Guvner comes in and says, 'What you doing with that stone?', *then* I'll have to think of an excuse. But I'm not worried until then. I think it's something to do with the way you're brought up. You either say, 'Oh, it's stealing, I don't want to know about it,' or you say, 'Oh, yeah, I'll have some of that.'

In circumstances in which a person is not particularly bothered about following the letter of the law, he may merely try to explain his crime in any way that protects him from the consequences of his law-breaking activity. It is well known that the way people explain questioned behaviour can affect the meaning it has for others and for themselves. Explanations, when they are given by law breakers, have traditionally been seen as attempts by the offender to protect himself from recrimination. The function of such an explanation 'is to alter the meaning that otherwise might be given to an act, transforming what could be seen as offensive into what could be seen as acceptable' (Goffman, 1971:139).

Numerous explanations are used by people to defend themselves. In many of these the person separates his *real self* from that part of him which committed the crime or broke the rule. For example, bringing people up to believe that they are not themselves when drunk allows them to see their drunken behaviour as an episodic happening which is not really associated with their true selves (MacAndrew and Edgerton, 1969). Thus, claiming one was drunk at the time of committing a crime is an acceptable excuse.

Separating the 'bad' part and accepting a momentary blow to one's moral character might work well as a defence if the offence in question is an infrequent occurrence. When the crime is committed often, it is necessary to develop a more all-embracing defence. For example, the professional fence interviewed by Carl Klockars said that it was no use assessing his 'bad' behaviour in isolation; it must be seen in the light of *total* past behaviour. He insisted that all the good things he had done must be taken into account in any character assessment. In the light of this, he said, he would 'come out on the good side' (Klockars, 1974:151). A similar kind of defence was found to exist among bread salesmen who fiddled their customers out of money. Jason Ditton said that these fiddlers developed 'part-time selves' through acting various characters which served as psychological and practical 'covers'. When questioned about their behaviour, they sustained the part-time fiddling self by drawing on a range of 'self-maintenance terminologies' such as 'It's the company that makes you what you are, because they're twisting us' (Ditton, 1977c:166).

The rationalisation of crimes may, however, become a more Machiavellian affair if the person involved *anticipates* that someone may question his behaviour. For manipulation to be successful, 'the offender must establish the credibility of his account by assuring its internal consistency and congruence with the facts. . . .' (Blumstein *et al.*, 1974:552). But as Steven Box (1971:130) points out, the offender may be sufficiently perceptive to see that those questioning him may see through any 'front' he might put up. To circumvent this vulnerability, he may alter his belief about his original intentions so that he can convince himself of his own innocence. Should his innermost thoughts be tapped, they would reveal that he was telling the 'truth'.

The chance of telling a convincing story can be increased in various ways. As well as claiming reduced responsibility or overall goodness, or fabricating a new biography, a person can assert his own guilt and reaffirm his allegiance to the law by showing remorse. To further enhance the likelihood of persuading those questioning him that he is really of good character, it may be necessary for the offender to employ lawyers to change or translate his beliefs into terms which are acceptable to those offended–as Scott and Lyman have argued:

The actual behaviour and beliefs of the actors in the untoward event in question are sometimes wrenched out of the original context and pressed into a Procrustean bed of publically acceptable action and morality. Abstruse legal rhetoric is itself used to mystify, so that the inevitable gaps between different value and belief positions in the conflictful pluralistic society will appear bridged. The language of law–like a magical incantation–creates the illusion of consistency and coherence. (Scott and Lyman, 1970:108)

So far I have only considered the possibility that the explanations offered by people are attempts to defend themselves *after* an act has been committed and subsequently questioned. There are those, however, whose commitment to conventional morality and law would normally prevent them from taking part in illegal activity in the first place. But if an acceptable account could be found in advance to rationalise the action, then the person could feel free to engage in it. C. Wright Mills was the first to recognise that the very explanations used by someone to defend himself, if applied before committing an act, though after contemplating it, could actually allow him to do it. Mills called this limited range of socially acceptable words and phrases for a given action the 'vocabulary of motives' (Mills, 1940;904). Later, in a study of financial trust violators, Donald Cressey confirmed Mills's hypothesis: 'I am convinced that the words the potential embezzler uses in his conversation with himself are actually the most important elements in the process which gets him into trouble or keeps him out of trouble' (Cressey, 1970:111). The single most important factor affecting the acceptability of offenders' accounts is whether they are seen as excuses or justifications.

The acceptability of explanations

Excuses are explanations through which a person accepts that the act in question is wrong but denies responsibility for it. He may, for example, say that he did not plan it but that it was decided for him; it was the result, perhaps, of an irresistable urge, an overwhelming temptation or an accident. Justifications are explanations through which the responsibility for the act is accepted but any 'wrongfulness' is denied. The person involved may assert the positive value of the act, saying that it was consciously planned, desirable and enjoyable (Scott and Lyman,

46

1970:180). Laurie Taylor's (1972) research into sex offenders, for example, showed that magistrates accorded significantly more credibility to explanations in which the offender did not assert any conscious control over his own behaviour, i.e. excuses. Less credibility was afforded to those who claimed that the action was intentional or justifiable.

In my study of amateur trading, the degree of credence given to the explanations of offenders was reflected in whether they were recommended for probation. In dealing with offenders, magistrates may request that the probation service undertake a social enquiry on the person concerned. On the basis of the probation officer's report, magistrates make decisions about the course of action that they will take. A senior probation officer explained, 'On the basis of the client's background and attitudes toward the offence, we form an opinion as to whether there was a causative factor present.' If it appears to be 'just cupidity', or succumbing to temptation combined with availability of goods, and if there are no problems meriting probation intervention, then probation officers report accordingly and 'the chances are it would be dealt with by a fine or imprisonment'. Another probation officer told me that when you reach the point of passing a professional opinion as to whether an individual is suitable for 'treatment', the recommendation depends upon the person's attitude.

> If you can see it's environmental and that probation won't stop it then you state that in your report. If a man comes in and says, 'I really want shot of this. I live in an environment where I can't stop it,' then that's a different matter. The probation could perhaps help inasmuch as you could be instrumental in having him rehoused in another area.

It would appear, therefore, that when the offender's explanation *coincides* with the probation officer's view of the 'cause' of the crime, in this case 'bad environment', then he is more likely to get 'treatment' than 'punishment'. Insofar as people are rewarded or punished not for what they do but for what they say, it is not surprising that 'men are often more interested in better justifying themselves, than in better behaving themselves' (Szasz, 1973:29).

Excuses and justifications

When asked about their involvement in the hidden economy and especially in amateur trading, people offer a range of excuses and justifications. Given the increasing acceptability of explanations like 'bad environment' or other broadly social 'causes', it is to be expected that such explanations should be offered in profusion. The most common of these explanations is the claim that various injustices of society are responsible for driving people to fiddle and deal. For example, John, a driver, who was unemployed at the time I spoke to him said, 'I'll tell you why a person does it. You try and make a decent living round here. I used to work for a hospital. I worked fifty, sixty and seventy hours a week and £44 was the most I got.' Dave, the builder, thought it was obvious why people were doing it: 'People on an assembly line, they've got all their debts to pay. Some are in arrears with the gas bills, the electricity bills. If something comes along, they're gonna have it.' He said, 'If they wanna call that dishonest, fair enough. I say that if they need the grub, then they ain't dishonest.'

For others, feeling relatively deprived is said to be the reason for becoming involved in fiddling. Derek said that most of the people in the rural area where he lived were unskilled labourers. 'They work in the pit, in forestry or on a farm. They know damn well they are being paid £19 a week and their employer is earning £30,000 a year from his farm. They'll have no qualms about a bag of fertiliser 'falling off' a trailer or 'losing' a rake or something like this.'

As well as citing inequalities of employment, people excuse their part-time criminal activity by making reference to how they are being tricked by everyone else, particularly the government. Molly, a cleaner I interviewed, said it was plainly the government's fault: 'You've got mortgages like they are, bloody food prices like they are and they're stopping wages and letting pensioners eat cardboard.' Lucy, the office worker, also felt that it was all the government's fault: 'The government blames

48

inflation but it's the government putting all the food into cold storage ready for the price rises.'

Others feel that, in general, the reasons for fiddling are an overall, inescapable pressure from industry and commerce. A man explained to *The Times* that

> People today feel they are being got at from all sides, particularly by commerce. From morning to night they are being bombarded with advertising slogans and high-pressure salesmanship. They get forced into buying things they don't want at prices they can't afford. Then when they get home, they find the goods are faulty anyway. They take their cars to garages and find the work charged for hasn't been done. They find the milkman starts delivering a kind of milk they haven't asked for just because he gets a bigger profit for it. Those things are happening to them all the time and it seems like they have no redress. So they get resentful and try to get their own back by stealing a little here and cheating a little there. Everyone else does it so why shouldn't they? (*The Times*, 1963:4)

With the injustices and trickery of society viewed as the reason for their poor economic position, people are taking the opportunity to buy 'cheap' in the spirit of Robin Hood. Molly explained that when people go to work they take bits to make up their wages. She said, 'I was talking to a man the other day and he says, "Molly, if I never fiddled, I would never be able to have any pocket money to go out because my wages would never stretch.' You could say he's robbin' them, but he don't see it as robbery because them bastards have robbed us in the beginning. So it's like a Robin Hood thing, 'ent it?' A writer for the magazine *Up Against the Law* summarized the feeling: 'Pilfering and fiddling are the "honest" response of millions of people to being exploited day in, day out, by employers. We are not stealing. We are taking back what is rightfully ours' (Up Against the Law Collective, 1974a:33). However, people do not explain their involvement in the hidden economy simply in terms of a *reaction* to certain social and environmental conditions. They also justify it to themselves in

49

relation to the general morality of other people.

A frequently expressed comment is 'everyone is doing it'. Molly felt certain that 'everyone of us has somewhere or other received property that's stolen. I don't think there is any of this about you don't know what you're receiving, 'cause you do.' Similarly, Sarah, a Birmingham factory worker, explained:

> Every single person on this earth has received something that's fell off the back of a lorry. Nobody could say they don't do it because they do. I don't know anybody who hasn't had furniture, washing machines, kitchen things. I don't know anybody who would say, 'Oh, I don't want it.' They'd all say, 'Ooh, can you get *me* one?' I tell you what–if you was to pinpoint all those who had had stuff and put them in a circle, you'd get 95 per cent of the population in that bloody circle.

Indeed, the belief that 'everyone is at it' can lead some, like Stan, to the conclusion that 'if it's offered I might as well take it because if I don't, someone else will.'

Molly felt strongly that 'people, reformers and everything, want to stop looking through their rose-coloured glasses, because the whole world is bent.' She said, 'Everybody has got their bloody fiddle.' However, rather than directing the attack at everyone, most people select particular groups who are supposed to represent upholders of morality. For example, Stan, the stonemason, who had done restoration work on a number of churches, did not hesitate to illustrate the statement 'no one is honest' with the example of the vicar who 'dips his hand in the collection box'. As he says, 'Now, you can't get much closer than a vicar for being honest, can you?'

Police, security men and all those connected with law enforcement are perhaps the most frequently cited moral hypocrites. Steve told me that in various places where he had worked, people 'took it for granted that coppers drop in for their weekly bung'. He felt that 'straight coppers' were 'few and far between'. Similarly, Margaret, a housewife whose husband was serving a prison term for handling stolen records, said, 'I don't give a damn what anybody thinks. I think the biggest criminals in this country are protected by the police until the

50

newspapers get hold of facts and information. Then it's wallop, they get it.' 'You offer a bargain to any policeman,' said Lucy, 'they're the biggest buyers. You offer them anything that's going and they'll have it.' The recent publicised evidence of police corruption serves to confirm these beliefs (Sherman, 1974; Cox *et al.*, 1977).

Like those concerned with law enforcement, businessman are also readily accused of various fiddles and deals. Dave illustrated the situation with hijacked lorry-loads of goods. 'It doesn't all go on one man's table, does it? It can't. It gets shunted around to shops, back into wholesale or to retail.' He explained how supermarket managers bought 'cheap' loads of meat in order to cover losses incurred as a result of their own fiddling. He also spoke of publicans arranging for 'thefts' of whisky, in order to 'cover' the occasions when they have dipped into Christmas Loan Club money. John explained that the real problem for shop managers arose when they were asked for stock checks after a theft. In order to cover their own fiddles, they increased the amount to be claimed from the insurance companies.

As other writers have pointed out, the largest group of people accused of fiddling in any particular workplace are the supervisors and managers. They are often said to encourage or cause other workers to start fiddling. Jason Ditton (1977c), for example, found that supervisors teach newly recruited bread salesmen to fiddle in order to avoid deductions from their wage packets as a result of mistakes made in collecting money from sales. During training the salesmen are told that the inevitable shortages can be pre-empted by overcharging customers for their bread. Once shown these techniques, the salesmen extend them for their own, rather than the company's, benefit.

> I'd ... put a penny on this, put a penny on that, you try it, then you think, 'Oh, well, that's two or three pounds extra in my pocket' ... that used to worry me at first ... but it isn't pennies now, it's pounds. (Ditton, 1977c:42)

In my own study, Lucy described how her husband, who works in the catering industry, began pilfering when he found 'higher-ups' doing it.

He's never taken anything in his life. You know how honest he's been. He's never brought anything home from work. I've always bought all my own bacon. Well, he discovered his boss one day. He kept saying, '*You* taking home bacon. But you don't *need* to take it. You've got a lovely house, a car, good wages and all the percentages on tips.' Well, after that he starts taking his own bacon. He starts bringing loads of it. I think it's become a disease now. Every time I come home there's a stack of it in the fridge. You've heard of collating, well, I file my bacon now in date order. I've got that way I don't buy it now. I just ask if he's got any more in.

So far then, I have argued that some people engaged in the hidden economy seek out acceptable excuses and justifications *in order* to rationalise their activity. As stated previously, such rationalisation may take place as a defence either after the act has been carried out, or after mere contemplation of it before taking part in the act. However, both of these interpretations assume that the person, for whatever reason, is already intent on a devious course and is merely making life more comfortable for himself. They assume, also, that the justifications are designed for self-defence in the case of, or during, questioning. But a third possible interpretation exists: the conversational words and phrases used by people in their daily life themselves neutralise any commitment to morality and this happens *before* the act in question is even contemplated.

NEUTRALISING MORALITY

It is possible that people's explanations of their activity are no more than selected, spoken aspects of a more general, pre-existing set of beliefs which allow crimes to be committed. Since researchers usually draw their material from interviews conducted after the event in question, it is difficult to know the extent to which an interviewee's account is designed to defend himself against the researcher's questions, or how much it is a reflection of an underlying set of general beliefs. Some indication that the explanations may reflect a pre-existing philosophy is apparent from the degree to which statements are related in the minds of the people involved. For example, it is possible to see a logical connection between the following statements: 'everyone is doing it', therefore 'no one is honest', which means 'everyone is dishonest' and, because of this, 'we are all being cheated'; our own action is, therefore, only 'taking back what is rightfully ours in the first place'. Such a philosophy would account, in part, for an ambivalent relationship with the law, as it allows a general support for broad legal principles. At the same time, it would exonerate those individuals whose feeling of being wronged justifies their 'getting their own back'. This kind of argument could be shown to have parallels with a Marxist political philosophy, according to which the 'capitalistic organisation of industry' is held responsible for people both feeling and being cheated. This philosophy regards the law as an instrument of the middle classes, designed to maintain the dominance of that class over all all others. The same philosophy justifies pilfering, fiddling and shoplifting in the following way:

> It's important who we nick from. If we nick from our friends we deserve to get done. We certainly don't deserve to have any friends. If we nick from a big supermarket we're doing nothing wrong. It's a crime to steal from your brothers and sisters; it's a public service to help each other nick from millionaire companies. (Up Against the Law Collective, 1974a:33)

However, it would be wrong to suggest that the majority of people who engage in the hidden economy do so because of some underlying Marxist philosophy. As Jason Ditton found among his bread salesmen, 'fiddling is not ... supported by a contra-culture' which opposes the main themes of society (Ditton, 1977c:173). The fiddling bread salesmen in Ditton's study do not believe that their activities will eventually overthrow the capitalist economy. The time will not come when mass rallies of fiddlers will protest their desire for eventual release from stigmatisation. Neither do other participants in the hidden economy see their action in a revolutionary way. As Molly, who herself had Marxist political sympathies, reflected:

> A lot of 'em don't think like that. We never used to think like that either. I never thought, 'Oh, well, they've already got it out of me.' I mean, you're gonna get a lot of people who don't have no political angle because they've got no bloody politics. They're not thinkin', 'Oh, well, they're robbin' us', they're thinkin', 'It's something cheap', and that's all it amounts to. We've got the money. We want it.

But the fact that 'all it amounts to' is 'something cheap' is significant in itself, for it suggests that the question of morality does not arise. This implies that any commitment to morality is either somehow neutralised in advance or does not exist in the first place.

David Matza was the first to appreciate that a person does not *deliberately* set out to short-circuit his moral inhibition against participating in criminal behaviour. He argues that justifications are inherent in society. Any rules that exist are not categorical imperatives but qualified guides for action. They are limited in their applicability by time, place, persons and social circumstances and, importantly, their limits are stated as conditions under which the rules are not binding. For example, someone who believes that the law should protect people from dishonesty may, at the same time, see nothing wrong in a 'technical infringement' of the law, if it does not involve particular people being hurt. As an assistant who worked for Michael in the hair stylist's said: 'I don't agree to stealing from small businesses. That's really bad. But if you see some Marks and Spencer's shirts with the labels cut out, you're not bothered. It doesn't hurt them. They've got enough that it doesn't matter if they lose a bit.' Where Matza differs from other theorists is in his assertion that 'neutralisation' is not an intentional or purposive act. In his opinion, it is something that occurs to the offender as a result of the unwitting duplication, distortion and extension of customary beliefs. As he says, 'Neutralisation of legal precepts depends partly on equivocation–the unwitting use of concepts in markedly different ways' (Matza, 1964:74).

In short, then, the concepts, words and phrases we use in our everyday conversation may themselves hide the illegality of the hidden economy and therefore render us unwitting participants in illegal acts. In particular, the language of legitimate business and commerce is probably more responsible than any other language for neutralising conventional morality.

The language of the market place

According to a recent government document, *Bargain Offer Claims*, an essential part of the consumer's purchasing decision is the search for the 'best bargain' (Office of Fair Trading, 1975:11). Many legitimate traders promote their goods by saying that their prices are reduced or are lower than those of other sellers. Quite obviously, this is to convince consumers that their products offer exceptionally good value for money. The report says that bargain-offer claims attempt to persuade consumers to buy now rather than later, and to buy these goods from them rather than similar or even different goods elsewhere. In making bargain-offer claims, a wide assortment of terms are used by media advertisers. Familiar phrases include 'Bargain price', 'discount offer', 'sale price', 'reduced price', special low price', bargain of the month', 'duty-free', 'special introductory offer', 'save up to 30%' and 'big discounts' (Office of Fair Trading, 1975:6). While the writers of the report feel that controls ought to be exercised over those claims which may mislead the public, they point out that most bargain-offer claims are 'a valuable promotional weapon'. Illustrative is its support for those that claim a reduction from the seller's previous price:

> ... they enable the seller to indicate a reduction or a 'sale', through which he can often achieve a temporary advantage over his competitors or can dispose of his surplus stock. They give the consumer a benefit because they provide an indication that—for the moment at least—the trader's terms are now more favourable, possibly better, than anyone else's and for society as a whole they promote price competition

which brings other wide, economic benefits. (Office of Fair Trading, 1975:13).

In short, the notion of bargain offers and cheap goods is a necessary part of the armoury of efficient consumers in our market economy.

From my research into the amateur trade in stolen goods, it was clear that the terms used in market-economy trading were extended to hidden-economy trading in such a way as to mask the unacceptable knowledge that the goods were actually stolen. As I stated at the beginning of this chapter, the law says that 'knowing or believing' goods are stolen renders the purchaser guilty of a criminal offence. Such knowledge could prevent someone who was committed to conventional morality from becoming involved. But unacceptable knowledge may be transformed into unobjectionable knowledge by the way in which people talk about what they do. Saying openly, or even to yourself, that you are buying 'cheap' goods, 'bargains' or, classically, 'stuff that's fallen off the back of a lorry', instead of 'stolen goods', makes it morally more acceptable and legally less dangerous. As Derek, the industrial designer, explained:

Most people actually have this belief within them that unless someone actually says, 'This has been nicked. Do you want it?', then they can choose to remain ignorant of the fact that it's been stolen, regardless of how stupendous the price or whatever, and therefore that protects them legally. I mean I know it doesn't but people feel this, and I think this is the reason for it, this question of protection. I think that the people are offered goods that they openly suspect to be stolen turn it down flat for that reason.

Not surprisingly then, people trading in stolen goods do not make the fact that their goods are stolen very clear. As Dave said, 'People don't come right out with it. They say, "I've got something a bit cheap here," or "Do you want a bargain?"' The words used never state the genuine origin of the goods. Michael, the hair stylist, explained that 'you don't kind of say "receiving" something. You say, "I can get cheap cigarettes

56

or tape recorders" or whatever. Only when you go into it further do you find out they are knocked off.' He said that he never tells people the goods are stolen.

I just say I got it from somewhere. They don't even ask really. I shouldn't think they even suspect half the time. They might know there's a fiddle somewhere along the line, but they don't know where. See, I sell it to them at slightly dearer than what they could get it if it was knocked off. This sort of price leaves it that the stuff needn't be stolen. They might be damaged goods or soiled or anything like that.

Typically, then, the goods are sold by ambiguous presentation; that is, the sale is accompanied by a gloss which relies on the fact that the purchaser will supply his own explanation of their origin. Occasionally, a complete sales story will accompany the goods, as in the following example of a friend of Steve's, who was selling 'cheap' salmon:

He was knocking out cases of it. He'd go round touting it at Lloyd's and these blokes would say, 'Oh, it's cheap, is it? I'll have some of that.' And everyone was slapping him on the back, saying what a great bloke he was because he could get cheap stuff. *He used to give them a yarn about his brother getting it cheap from the cash-and-carry.* [My emphasis]

With goods presented in this way, a person may feel morally free to go ahead and make a purchase. As Lucy, the office clerk, recounted:

If somebody came along and said to me, 'This is stolen goods. Do you want it?' I wouldn't want to know. No, thanks. I wouldn't take it. But if they said, 'It's off the back of a lorry,' I wouldn't mind. I don't think I'd like to know if they were stolen. I'd like to kid myself it was allright. I wouldn't like to know it was pinched. I wouldn't like it right out. It might enter the back of my mind but

57

provided they didn't tell me straight to my face I would try and avoid the issue there. I'd say, 'I'd like it very much.'

A potentially embarrassing piece of information, which threatens to disturb this state of unawareness, is the price of the goods. As Molly explained, 'If somebody came along and said, "I've a coffee pot to sell and I only want two quid for it", and you'd seen them same coffee pots for twenty-three quid in Marks and Spencers, you know in your own bloody mind that's not a straight coffee pot, but you want to *believe* it because you're after a bargain.' In order to account for the cheapness of stolen goods, and therefore to allow their stolen nature to remain hidden, a range of explanations is used. Many of these are extensions of conventionally held beliefs which explain the sale of legitimate bargains. Statements to the effect that the goods have 'fallen off the back of a lorry' are now synonymous with an acknowledgement that the goods are stolen. Nevertheless, other more plausible explanations are available.

In explanations of their cheap price, goods may be described as being of poor quality. For example, they may be seconds or rejects: 'Like those knives,' said Lucy. 'They were rejects. I think a lot of his stuff is inferior quality.' Alternatively, goods may be described as 'damaged in transit': 'Like you can get tins of peaches cheap at the supermarket because they're dented,' declared a publican indicted on a charge of buying cases of stolen whisky from a supermarket manager. 'Damage' may be the product of shop-soiling or the result of a fire, as Molly knew well: 'You can go into some warehouses and buy up and take away stocks of dresses and coats, cheaply and all above board, because maybe they've been pulled out of a fire.' A similar explanation may be that the goods are perishable. Meat and vegetables, for example, 'have to be sold' before they go rotten. Goods may be spoken of as 'left-overs', as in the case recounted by a probation officer, who told me about 'off-cuts' of carpets that 'ran into a hundred square yards'. The ingenuity of explanations for the cheapness of goods in terms of poor quality can be quite remarkable, as when Lucy asked me about portable televisions for 'fifty bob'. 'What

58

could a TV be like for fifty bob? I should think they're battery driven and the batteries cost more than the TV.'

The quality of the goods is only one way of accounting for a bargain price. Another is to claim that the goods are cheap because they have been purchased in bulk, thus entitling the buyer to a discount. 'If you buy large amounts, you can get it that much cheaper, so it needn't be stolen. They *might* have got it that way. I'm not to know,' said Lucy. She felt that it was the same as buying from warehouses or from a discount store: 'It's got to be cheaper because there's no middle-man.' Yet a further explanation of cheap prices is that the goods might be legitimate perks; ordinary payments in kind which are allowed because a person works in a particular place: 'Like vegetables from the market. If you work in a market, you can get all your vegetables free. But it's perks like tips.' Molly agreed: 'It's part of the perks of the bloody job; you take that just to make your little bit of wages up.'

When goods are ambiguously presented, it is not surprising that many people draw on their stock of purchasing knowledge gained as legitimate consumers, and resolve the ambiguity in a way which unwittingly masks the illegality of the purchase. The goods in question become 'bargains' and 'everyone wants a bargain'. Steve said, 'Everyone's happy to get something cheap if they can.' Stan thought that, 'if someone's offered a *bargain* ... if they was in their right mind they'd have it. I should think 99 per cent of people would, in their right mind.' A probation officer I interviewed commented, 'Well, we live in a consumer society, don't we? You know, if you come in with a lot of nice vases and curtains and fishing rods and electrical goods and things like this. It's all goods, isn't it, possessions, commodities, things? They might not be any use to you but you have 'em and there you are, you see.' But the casual nature of the trade in which there is apparently nothing criminally significant in buying cheap goods was best expressed by Steve, who told me at the beginning of our interview, 'The kind of trading I know about is just part of everyday life, of going to work and coming home, where everyone is happy to get a bargain.'

An equally serious way in which the illegality of crime is

neutralised, occurs not as a result of our use of market economy words and phrases, but as a result of the way criminal stereotypes are used in trying to deter crime. In the next chapter I will show how part-time trading has been presented as a criminal enterprise by commentators who have succeeded in creating, first, the public image of the fence and, latterly, the stereotype of the fence as the Mr Big of property crime. Ironically, this stereotype, rather than deterring potential amateur dealers, can be shown actually to neutralise ordinary people's moral commitment in such a way that illegal behaviour is seen as 'not that bad'.

4. Criminal Stereotypes and Moral Freedom

> *The fact of reportage alone cannot provide the necessary potency to arouse and reaffirm public support and recognition of the moral boundaries of society.* Only where there is a public pronouncement of the offence, drawing out its illegality and immorality, are moral boundaries reaffirmed and individually reinforced. But such pronouncements do not follow simply from the *fact* of a crime being committed ... The reason why deviant behaviour occupies so much media space is not because it is intrinsically interesting, but because it is intrinsically constructive. It serves to reinforce the world-taken-for-granted by restating social rules and warning subjects that violators will not be tolerated.
>
> *Steven Box* (1971:39)

In their efforts to control public morality it has been traditional practice for crime reporters and commentators to concentrate their attention on portraying stereotypical images of the full-time criminal. The history of hidden-economy trading has not escaped this process. It is dominated by three interrelated themes: a refusal by contemporary writers to pay any serious attention to amateur activity or part-time 'dishonesty'; a tendency to see all part-time crime as fundamentally criminal; and a concentration of all public discussion on the evils of the professional criminal. In recent years, attempts have been made to strengthen the stereotype of the trader in stolen goods. He has been transformed from an underworld supporter of theft to a businessman-dealer who organises, and is the brains behind, theft. Ironically, however, the creation of the fence as crime's Mr Big has itself helped to foster the ambivalent morality of participants in the hidden economy.

THE ORIGINAL IMAGE: RECEIVERS

The law against receiving stolen property is a good measure of how trading in stolen goods was originally seen. In F. L. Attenborough's *Laws of the Earliest English Kings*, there is reference to the law against 'harbouring stolen cattle', which was one of Ine's laws of about AD 690 (Attenborough, 1922:51). But it was for receiving 'bad men' rather than goods that the law was originally formulated. Jerome Hall quotes laws of the Middle Ages, saying that:

> ... if anyone has knowingly fed such a person after his outlawry and expulsion and received and held communication with him in any way, or harboured or concealed him, he ought to be punished with the same punishment with which the outlaw is punished. (Hall, 1952:53)

Indeed, up until 1602 it was not illegal to receive goods, but it was an offence to receive the felon. Until 1691, under Common Law, receiving stolen goods was only a misdemeanour, punishable by a fine or whipping, but in that year a statute of William III and Mary II made the receiver an accessory after the fact and liable to branding, whipping and/or seven years' transportation (Act 3 and 4, William and Mary c.9.s.4; Howson, 1970:36).

Indeed, it is the case that up until 1702 prosecution of the receiver was not possible unless the thief was first apprehended and then convicted. It was not until 1822, after pressure had been exerted by law reformers, that an act, revised under George IV (Act 7 and 8, Geo. IV c.29) in 1827, made provision for the independent trial of the receiver, whose offence was made a felony regardless of whether or not the thief was first arrested. While there was no strict law against receiving stolen goods prior to the seventeenth century, it was recognised that the activity went on and that it was as bad as theft, which it may actually cause. For example, in 1592 Robert Greene said that receivers of stolen goods were 'as pernicious as the lift [thief]'.

> Thus are these brokers and bawds, as it were efficient causes of the lifter's villainy, for, were it not for their alluring speeches and their secret concealings, the lift, for want of receivers, should be fain to take a new course of life, or else be continually driven to great extremes for selling his garbage. (Greene, 1592:171)

But the overriding theme throughout both the history of theft law and contemporary writing is that the crime of theft is helped and supported by the receiver of either 'bad men' or 'garbage' (stolen goods). Indeed, it was this conception of the *passive* supporting role of receivers that informed the cant expression 'fence'. This word derives from the standard English 'to protect', as in the word 'defence', and represents protection for the thief against being caught in possession of the stolen goods (Partridge, 1968:542). Support could range from giving the person a place of hiding to 'converting' his stolen goods into cash. So great was the dominance of this way of seeing things that, even though striving to change the law prior to 1822, Patrick Colquhoun, in his major *Treatise on the Police of the Metropolis*, could only see the thief as *dependent* on the receiver. Echoing Greene, he proclaimed:

> There can be little hesitation in pronouncing the Receivers to be the most mischievous of the whole; in as much as without the aid they afford, in purchasing and concealing every species of property stolen or fraudulently obtained, Thieves, Robbers and Swindlers as already observed must quit the trade as unproductive and hazardous in the extreme ... Nothing can be more just than the old observation, that, 'if there were no receivers there would be no Thieves'—Deprive

a thief of the sale and ready-made market for his goods and he is undone. (Colquhoun, 1795:289)

The idea that the thief was being supported by the receiver of stolen goods was undoubtedly a relic of the time when he befriended 'bad men'. I believe it was based on an erroneous assumption that people would not steal without having somewhere to 'dispose' of the 'garbage'. In contrast to the reforming opinion of Colquhoun and others, who were the exception rather than the rule, Thomas Dudley wrote in his 1828 review of the London police establishments:

The common phrase 'if there were no receivers there would be no thieves' in my opinion should be quite reversed; if there were no thieves there would be no receivers. I am for *preventing* which is much better than to *cure*. Supposing there were no receivers to melt the plate, take watches or jewellery to pieces etc., do you think the thieves have not ingenuity enough to put a common crucible in the fire, cut the gold or silver plate to pieces and melt it and pour it out into an ingot? Where is there a refiner in London who would not buy it in that state and how is the identity to be proved? (Dudley, 1828:39)

Overall, even by the mid-nineteenth century, very little concern was expressed about the influence of receiving on the structure of property theft. I contend that the reason for this was a simple one. Receiving or trading in stolen goods was, generally speaking, not deemed important, because to have claimed that it was would have meant accepting that someone could both be involved in illegal activity and a legitimate member of society. The implications of this would not have been compatible with the contemporary conception of the morality of society. Instead, the idea was developed of the receiver as a *supporter* of thieves, as a functioning part in a system of theft, though nearly always a lesser character than the thieves themselves.

By the late eighteenth and early nineteenth century, even when evidence was available that the fence could have a more central and active role, no general attempt was made to acknowledge such evidence. The activities of Jonathan Wild, who ruled London's underworld between 1715 and 1725, should have shown contemporary writers that the receiver's role in the theft of property could be more than supportive, but they did not interpret it in this way. They failed to see that the practices of combining business in stolen goods with 'thief-taking' (an early form of policing which Wild used to his advantage as the self-styled Thief-Taker General of Great Britain and Ireland) were open to anyone with a source of stolen goods. Even the Act of 1718 (4, George I c.II, sec. 485) which, in 1725, was used to send Wild to the gallows, was seen as a measure specifically designed to deal with him rather than with the matter as a whole. Wild was portrayed as an exception rather than as a typical case. As Gerald Howson said, 'Just though it may have been, Wild's death taught no lessons, brought no reforms, and alleviated no suffering' (Howson, 1970:283).

The precise state of the interpretation of receiving at the beginning of the nineteenth century is best expressed by Colquhoun. He divided receivers of stolen property in the 'Metropolis' into two main classes:

1. The Dealers connected with professed and notorious thieves and who are their principal supporters ... Many of these have, themselves, been originally thieves ... who prefer to conceal the fraud, frequently set up Chandlers' shops, Coal Sheds, Potatoe-Warehouses or Old Iron Shops and not seldom become masters of public houses, that they may appear to have some visible means of obtaining a livelihood.
2. The Dealers in Old Iron and other Metal-Rags-Old Wearing Apparel-Buyers, Refiners and makers of gold and silver— Dealers in Secondhand Furniture and Building Materials and that class of Pawnbrokers who have connections with criminal people. ... (Colquhoun, 1795:292)

But he also included two additional kinds of receiver: 'Innocent Receivers', who are not aware that they are purchasing stolen articles, and 'Careless Receivers', who ask no questions and purchase everything that is offered. He subsequently called the latter 'Covetous Receivers', and described as 'Careless Receivers', those who, 'without meditating evil design, purchase indiscriminately whatever they can obtain cheap, under the idea that it is a private adventure . . .' (Colquhoun, 1800:195).

This typology of criminals was a significant change from earlier reports, in which receivers were depicted as either wholly supportive underworld figures or once-in-a-lifetime criminal entrepreneurs. Interestingly, Colquhoun retained the notion that the sole purpose of the trader's legitimate business was that of a 'cover' for his 'nefarious' activity. To this end, he largely included lower-class traders, such as Jewish secondhand dealers, pawnbrokers and scrap-metal merchants. Nevertheless, in the course of his two treatises he had introduced a whole range of 'middle-class' traders which he said were also associated with buying stolen goods. Among Colquhoun's categories of receivers were sugar refiners, purchasers of tea, coffee, hemp ashes and timber, grocers, metal merchants, chandlers, publicans, and manufacturers of twine and ropes (Colquhoun, 1800:194). These new classes of fence were to have serious implications for the way receiving was regarded.

The revelation or admission, by the first quarter of the nineteenth century, that a higher class of businessman was involved in trading in stolen goods marked a turning-point in the public debate, which dismayed some people at the time. In his review of London police establishments, Thomas Dudley admitted the fact:

> I am sorry to say there have been tradesmen to all appearances respectable, who, for the sordid lucre of gain and avariciousness, have sacrificed their integrity and credit by engaging in this shameful traffic while, at the same time, they have been doing well in an honourable way of business . . . There are many tradesmen of respectability who purchase goods not exactly in their business, in a loose manner. . . . (Dudley, 1828:38)

Another writer wrote a series of articles for *Frazer's Magazine* in which, as well as listing the now usual range of Jewish pawnbrokers, marine store owners, general dealers, washerwomen and 'women who kept stalls in the street', he added a category

66

of 'many very large and wealthy houses in the City of London whose transactions of late years can come under no other denomination. . . .' (anonymous, 1832:491). He also raised the question of how it was that these 'receivers of stolen goods are not more exposed? Is it because they all become so rich and by the modern gauge of respectability are influential and company for gentlemen?' (anonymous, 1832:493).

Clearly, there was no longer any real credibility in pretending that dealing in stolen goods was the sole province of full-time criminals, ex-thieves or, for that matter, servants, employees and lower-class traders. But how the implications of this evidence were handled was extremely interesting. It should have entailed the admission that 'honest' people were not so 'honest' after all, or that, in fact, there was no such thing as a category of 'honest' people. Instead, it resulted in an amplification of the stereotype for this type of crime.

THE STEREOTYPE OF THE PROFESSIONAL FENCE

A new, two-part explanation emerged in the public debate. First, a distinction was made between the lesser forms of receiver and the other, more important, traders that were called professionals. In 1865, an author distinguished between 'occasional receivers', who were 'by no means the pillars of the trade', and 'the professional receiver', or 'fence-master'. Fence-masters were men of almost every variety of character and circumstance: 'Broken tradesmen, dishonoured clerks, and quondam thieves; men of some education and men of none, but all of them fond of money and many of them respectable in their appearance and temperate in their habits' (anonymous, 1865:129). According to his reckoning, there were three classes of fence-master: 'No. 3', who lives with thieves, 'No. 2', who lives near thieves, and 'No. 1'.

No. 1 fence-master is the .top of the guilty profession, the Bank of England for Thievdom and the most pernicious rascal unhung. He has plenty of money and follows the guilty trader from sheer love of wickedness and gain ... And yet, this sleek hypocrite—wrongfully accused according to his own account—is one of the cleverest and most systematic members of the whole criminal fraternity ... The police have no means of knowing this class of criminal, and how the evil is to be grappled with we cannot tell. (anonymous, 1865:130)

He might not have known what line of defence to adopt, but creating a mythical arch criminal type, the 'No. 1 fence-master', was a good way to start. Isolating and separating the professional fence as the Mr Big of property crime and demonstrating that many occasional receivers were unwitting or careless, restored the idea that there were a few major criminals, while everyone else was honest. To complete the picture, a second part of the explanation was provided to account for the equally disturbing fact that all the stolen goods ended up in honest hands. The simple answer was that 'stolen goods pass through many hands' and get progressively less contaminated as the goods move out into 'honest life' (anonymous, 1865:130).

The difference between occasional receivers and the professional fence was further developed in America at about this time. Writing in *The Galaxy*, Edward Crapsey spelled out the revitalised attack on the newly conceived professional fence:

In New York, as in all other great commercial cities ... it might be shown that the receiver who is the manufacturer of thieves is worse than his product ... it is evident that there are no criminals more deserving of public attention than these fences, without whom the rogues would be an army without arms. (Crapsey, 1871:494)

While Crapsey used the explanation about professional fences working stolen goods 'back into channels of legitimate trade', he also included a far more realistic assessment of the situation than had any of his English contemporaries. He said that fences had no difficulty in working off their illicit stock as they knew that 'there are many men engaged in business which seems legitimate, who are ready at any time to dabble in anything that promises a profit'. He went on to say that cases were constantly coming up in sufficient numbers 'to prove the readiness of a large class of businessmen to buy anything which can be sold at a bargain. . . .' (Crapsey, 1871:502).

In addition, unlike anyone else at the time, Crapsey at least partly learned the lesson of Jonathan Wild, that there are 'many flagrant cases of collusion between the police and plunderers' and also between police and receiver. He says that there are two major problems that may arise, not least of which is that 'it is to the interest of everybody that the case shall not go to court; the owner wants his property, the policeman his reward, and the fence impunity. . . .' Because of these facts, says Crapsey, 'dealing in stolen goods has become and threatens to permanently remain, one of the leading industries of the metropolis' (Crapsey, 1871:502).

Not only was Crapsey relatively perceptive in his view of the professional fencing business, and of how the 'professional' legitimised both his goods and himself (Henry, 1977), but his account of what he called occasional or 'casual receivers' was the most elaborate to date. Crapsey confirmed Colquhoun's original observation that there were many who occasionally dealt in stolen goods, saying that they 'practically were fences *and yet do not exclusively devote themselves to the pursuit'*. He said these people bought chiefly from:

> . . . dishonest clerks who cheat their employers out of small articles of stock . . . porters or truckmen who pilfer from the goods entrusted to their care or who obtain articles from business associates or their employers; as if a clerk should go to a house with which his master is in the habit of dealing and order a bill on account of his employer and take the goods to the fence and sell them on his own account. This species of crime is of daily occurrence. . . . (Crapsey, 1871:499)

The implications of Crapsey's evidence indicated that numerous businessmen were dealing on the side with apparently honest employees. However, succeeding writers interpreted this differently.

The casual, occasional, careless and covetous receiver was

a useful character to have in any classification of traders in stolen property, since he afforded an ideal medium through which honest people came by their bargains. But the dominant figure in the emerging scenario was the 'professional businessman-fence'. If apparently legitimate businessmen with 'good education' and a gentlemanly background were involved, then they fitted neither into the underworld, being too clever for it, nor into the majority of the population, being too dishonest for it. Their natural place was at the top: the key figures in the property theft business.

The fence as crime's Mr Big

Thus, the view of trading in stolen goods emerged according to which the professional fence was stereotyped as the principal felon in property theft. The professional fence was not simply a tool of his supplier, nor did he passively offer protection and services. Rather, he was the main protagonist in the business operation of theft in which the thief was little more than his instrumental employee. The professional fence was seen as actively training, recruiting, organising and controlling thieves. In an April 1926 *New York Herald-Tribune* article entitled 'Swift Punishment of Crafty "Fences" seen as Key to War on Theft', John Walker Harrington said that the old-time Fagin character was 'put to shame by the modern ilk'.

It was the old theory of the law that the receiver of stolen goods was merely the tool of the bolder thief. Indeed, this idea seems to have obtained until the beginning of the last century ... Certainly, according to all recent developments in the history of crime, the fence is a worse criminal than the hold-up man or the burglar.... (Harrington, 1926:3)

Harrington insisted that in all property theft transactions, 'the real instigator', the professional fence, 'is the invisible master of the show, pulling the strings which move the puppets of crime'.

Five months later, the *New York Times* carried a full-page

70

piece in which Edward H. Smith endorsed Harrington's position, seeing the fence as the real 'master-mind'. He argued that crime had now evolved as big business, asserting that from 'the petty thief to fence, the underworld has built up and ably directed far-reaching organisation with its tentacles reaching out into commercial, political and social realms' (Smith, 1926:5).

By 1928, the Prison Committee of the Association of Grand Jurors of New York County had produced the first-ever book on fencing, entitled *Criminal Receivers in the United States*. In his preface to the book, Thomas Rice pointed out that 'only in the last few years in the whole history of crime, which is as old as civilisation, has the seriousness of receiving stolen goods been recognised'(Rice, 1928:ix). He concluded by saying that 'the layman, the lawyer, the legislator and, above all, the judge, have been beguiled into an utterly false conception of [the fence's] vital importance in the problem of crime ... have little understood the status of the fence as a promoter of theft' (Rice, 1928:xii).

Significantly, in all this myth creation vital components of the trade in stolen goods had been lost. Gone was the co-operation between the businessman-fence and the police. Also missing was the man in an honest job who traded with the fence. An article on stolen goods by Courtney Ryley Cooper in the *Saturday Evening Post* of 1936 attributed a great part of America's crime bill to the competition of stolen goods with legitimate business. He was in favour of the new belief that 'the man who foists (stolen goods) upon otherwise honest citizens is a bigger crook than the man who steals them' (Cooper, 1936:16). He also maintained that the generally accepted picture of the average fence must change from that of a creature of the underworld, 'subsisting on petty larceny', to one 'in which he is friends of law and and order': 'Nowhere is this fence a skulking habitué of dives and dens, but an integral part of the ordinary run of society' (Cooper, 1936:69).

The culmination of the new view of fencing was Jerome Hall's now classic study of receiving (Hall, 1952), in which he pressed for law reform to take into account the professional businessman-fence. He criticised the legal conception of the 'receiver', saying that the law 'selects as crucial one small segment of the socially significant behaviour, namely receiving, which is not even the most important characteristic of this type of behaviour' (Hall, 1952:155). The fence was seen by Hall as a dealer first and foremost, for whom buying was only one small part of his activities 'just as with any merchant'. More importantly, Hall argued that the traditional approach of the law did not differentiate between the behaviour of non-professional offenders and that of the dealer—a distinction he thought essential. Hall, like his predecessors, felt it was necessary to include part-time operators in his typology. He identified two types of 'non-professional', the 'lay receiver' who purchases stolen goods for his own consumption, and the 'occasional receiver' who purchases stolen goods 'for resale', but 'infrequently' (Hall, 1952:155). The problem, Hall said, was that the ultimate consumer was included in the same category as the professional receiver 'who buys for resale and not for consumption'.

Hall's classification of receivers is important because, as with those of his predecessors, it was used as a technique for creating an illusory distinction which enabled him to throw into relief the criminal identity of the professional fence, a dealer in stolen goods, controller of thieves, arch-criminal and a primary focus for attention. At the same time, his framework left the general population free of guilt; either entirely innocent, or guilty of only a minor offence. However, we need not merely suppose that Hall is deluding us, for he tells us that, in order to 'simplify' the problem, he omits the 'intermediate groups' of persons who buy occasionally for resale. He argues, 'Even if it were true that receivers cannot be sharply divided, this would not affect the problem of treating the extremes differently, i.e. the need to construct at least two broad classes' (Hall, 1952:218). In fact, if the intermediate groups were recognised as comprising the major portion of the population, this would not just affect the problem, it would transform it. Unfortunately, however, so powerful was Hall's analysis, that most recent research merely elaborates his interpretation.

For example, Duncan Chappell and Marilyn Walsh argue that the conventional view of theft, which concentrates exclusively on the thief, draws the boundaries of crime too tightly around

72

that individual. They maintain that theft is only the beginning of an intricate process by which stolen property is acquired, converted, redistributed and reintegrated into a legitimate property stream: 'The thief becomes little more than an instrument of the fence—a highly visible but relatively minor cog in a gigantic distribution circuit.' They call this the 'Stolen Property System', which they define as 'that set of individuals *and their interactions* which locates, plans, facilitates and executes the extraction of goods from one owner and its transfer to a new owner' (Chappell and Walsh, 1974:115).

It is my contention, then, that the fence, as he is now portrayed, is misrepresented. I believe that, because of the nature of the evidence used, commentators have made serious omissions in their explanation of how the fence operates but, importantly, they have also constructed a false picture of the amateur trade.

The other side of the fence

Carl Klockars, in his book *The Professional Fence*, criticises Hall's typology as being unsatisfactory in the way it depicted both part-time and full-time dealing in stolen goods. He says Hall took the idea—the image of the professional—too seriously.

> Hall, himself a professional, must surely have known that professionals, even learned ones, are not nearly so rational nor disciplined nor perfectly formidable as they let outsiders believe they are ... Hall might have added other factors: the competence of the receiver, his business acumen, the attention he gives to his work, his industry or indolence, the condition of his health, his relationship with his wife, the intonation of his voice, and the quality of his best manipulative smile. But Hall's image of the professional is ideal. It admits no bungling, no stupidity, no laziness, no poor judgement, no misunderstandings, no pathos and no humour. (Klockars, 1974:169)

In contrast, Klockars describes his businessman-fence, 'Vincent', as a fun-loving human character who, rather than simply making money or accumulating personal wealth, enjoys a certain creative satisfaction from his 'wheeling and dealing'. Vincent enjoys his work. He also enjoys other activities surrounding the exchange of stolen goods. Klockars describes how on Sundays Vincent is host to local businessmen, providing them with coffee and doughnuts as refreshments while together they 'review last week's triumphs and discuss this week's opportunities' (1974:76), and he recounts how the arrival of distinguished people, or those Vincent has known for many years, prompts a minor celebration (1974:105). He emphasises that Vincent is liked by the people he does business with (in contrast to the traditionally held view that hostility exists between 'fence' and 'thief'); that, if it were otherwise, recriminations would be evident and they are not. Perhaps most interestingly, Klockars shows that his fence is as much a part of legitimate society as any other businessman. Vincent makes large donations to civic and charitable activities, which include orphanages, churches, delinquency and recreational programmes, firemens' and other public service funds, estimated in total as equivalent to a yearly $10 million tax saving (Klockars, 1974:193).

However, in my view, the most fundamental criticism of Hall made by Klockars was that he 'did not take the amateur trade seriously enough'. He says Hall's 'images of the lay and occasional receivers are widely sparse and flat. They suggest nothing of the trade in stolen property among amateur thieves and dabbling dealers which thrives in bars, schools, offices, factories and neighbourhoods' (1974:169).

THE CONTROL PARADOX OF CRIMINAL STEREOTYPES

Dominating the historical commentary on crime in general and any specific illegal activity is an attempt to separate, isolate and stigmatise the offender. For those members of society who were its self-appointed moral guardians, and who felt the need to maintain the social rules to 'bring together upright consciences and concentrate them' (Durkheim, 1947), attempting to get the wayward to return was of no avail. The only course was for them to reject the unacceptable, to cut them off from the so-called honest population. However, as Steven Box has pointed out, it is not criminal behaviour as such which is responsible for arousing the moral and aesthetic sentiments of the public, but a particular kind of response to it. Criminal stereotypes were a simple way of pronouncing publically on an offence and of indicating its illegality and immorality. So hostile was the moral condemnation of anyone committing an illegal offence, that all sight of the real relationship of their crimes to their jobs and the rest of their lives was lost. The commentary, at least up to the mid-nineteenth century, was so moralistic that all degrees of crime, all subtlety and shading were obscured. There was no allowance for occasional 'dishonesty' and certainly not for regular 'small-time' dishonesty. A man who broke the law was a criminal, pure and simple.

Thus, by classifying offenders into criminal types (delinquents, thieves, fences), by talking of criminal classes (the underworld, the rookeries, the 'low life') and of gangs and syndicates, rather than seeing offending as part of ordinary people's lives, the commentators on crime effectively created the notion of a parasitic counter-culture, motivated by greed and lust with its own 'depraved and 'corrupt' ways and even its own language, a criminal cant. Because of its very nature, however, hidden-economy crime presented problems for the simple analysis. It was an anomaly; certainly not at ease among the honest population and yet not heinous enough to be employed by them as a negative stereotype in the public condemnation of crime. By definition it contradicted the clear assertion that men were either good and honest or bad and dishonest. It was the grey area between these extremes.

For the contemporary writers, the solution to this problem was simple; if a man in an honest job committed an offence, then that showed he was dishonest and if he was dishonest he must have taken the job in order to commit the offence. The formula could be applied directly to pilfering and fiddling from work because of the basic belief that servants or employees were untrustworthy anyway, being both envious and jealous of their master's/employer's situation. But it rested less well with 'amateur' trading. The trader or businessman who bought and sold stolen as well as legitimate goods was difficult to categorise. Here was a man who was obviously not easily dismissed as lower-class. He had some money. He was often well educated. He was able to conduct a legitimate business of sorts, which suggested he was on par with 'gentlemen'. But he was also engaged in crime. This anomalous character clearly threatened to undermine the whole mythology of the distinction between 'upright' men and criminals. As we have seen, this dilemma emerged in the nineteenth century because of the need felt by law reformers to control theft more effectively. It was resolved by designating the businessman-dealer the Mr Big of all property crime.

Ironically, however, this concentration of public debate on the stereotype of the full-time criminal not only fails to portray accurately those who actually make a living from crime, but also provides a stock of concepts which serve to trivialise the activities of part-time practitioners. Rather than seeing on-the-side dishonesty as bad, wrong, indicative of a criminal identity, the belief prevails that even though a person may be breaking the law himself, he is not doing anything really dishonest. Ditton has called this the diminishing return of classical crime stereotypes. He says, sardonically: 'Generally the mediated stereotype is so effective that even the most promising candidates fail to identify with it. It becomes ironic that middle-aged and light-fingered women just cannot see themselves as 'shoplifters'.' (Ditton, 1976a:431) And he quotes George Orwell: 'I imagine there are quite a lot of tramps who thank God they are not tramps. They are like trippers who say such cutting things about trippers' (Orwell, 1933:176). The difference between what ordinary people do 'on the side' and what full-time criminals do according to their stereotypical image is extremely clear to those people who are poised to become involved in the hidden economy.

Three fundamental distinctions are made by members of the hidden economy by which they contrast their own 'insignificant' behaviour with the 'really villainous' activity of the professional criminal. It is argued, for example, that whereas 'criminals' behave in a predatory way, ordinary people, in contrast, need only accept things that 'come their way'. A number of the

76

people I interviewed made a sharp distinction between 'going out and doing something' and accepting 'good fortune' that might come their way. Stan, the stonemason, for example, distinguished between stealing and pilfering in the following way:

> There are two different sorts of stealing. I wouldn't go out and break into somewhere and nick something. That's stealing. That's bad. You know, like the bloke who actually goes out and does it for a living, like breaking into somewhere and nicking a lorry-load of stuff. See, the people who steal that I know of are stealing from their works, their factories or garages. They are pilfering the odd box of this or box of that. They don't consider that wrong really. That's perks to them.

A further distinction made between hidden economy and full-time crime in the minds of ordinary people is the scale of operation. In the course of conducting interviews for the amateur trading study, I was continually told that the activity of the person I was interviewing was only 'small-time stuff' and not a fraction of what some people were doing. More than once I was told to 'go to where it's really at'. A good example of the distinction between what *he* did and what the *real* criminals were doing was given by Michael, the hair stylist: 'See, there are two channels to it. There's the small stuff where nothing's being made on it; and there's the big stuff.' He said that the 'small stuff' goes on with the 'little person doing a fiddle in the factory. But the big stuff ... goes to the customer through the proper channels, through the shops and back that way.'

However, the most significant contrast made between the public stereotype of full-time crime and the hidden economy is the fact that real crime provides the basic source of income for those involved. It is this, rather than any other aspect of the criminal stereotype, that renders a person morally free to commit part-time crime. People in ordinary, honest jobs know that they do not have to fiddle, pilfer or deal in order to earn a living. Thus, Stan describes how, for him, the money is not important:

77

I just think of the money I get from doing it as just pocket money. It's a couple of quid in my pocket. It's a little bit extra that helps you with the family, takes you on holiday that little bit further, lets you have an extra bit of luxury. But I don't need it. I can do without that money. It's different 'cause I'm not doing it for a living.

The importance of not participating in part-time crime for the money is so great, in some cases, that people draw up new moral boundaries for themselves. Rather than being committed to a counter-culture, or oppositional culture, they form their own personal moral sense of what is right and wrong. Often the borderlines of such personal moralities do not coincide with legal borderlines. In these cases, as Derek, the industrial designer, pointed out, 'There is a very narrow line between big business and crime, and the whole lot stinks.' Personal morality rests on doing things to help other people. The result of such reasoning is that a person can arrive at the conviction that part-time crime is actually *more* moral than most legitimate business. Derek was particularly clear on this point.

You know, you can talk a lot about what is legal and what isn't. To my mind this is probably technically illegal. Morally it isn't, because nobody is making money out of it . . . not real money. Well, allright, the person who's receiving the goods is saving money if you like, but he's not actually making anything. He's not going out selling the stuff . . . hawking it around, making a profit on it, not in actual money. And the bloke who is selling, he's not making much out of it. He's getting favours more than anything. It's not a business . . . or a shady business deal as such. It's sort of a community action group. But they wouldn't see it like that . . . they wouldn't understand it in those terms. They just do it. At this level it doesn't seem to multiply at all. You know, it doesn't get any worse or any more rampant. It works well . . . very well, and it helps the people a lot. You know, from that point of view it is just not immoral . . . I think in fact it's very, very moral. I think it's a good thing.

78

We can see, therefore, that the actual descriptive process used to control crime, in particular the use of criminal stereotypes, might be extended in such a way as to make otherwise morally committed people feel free to engage in illegal acts. However, before it is assumed that the use of criminal stereotypes by members of the hidden economy is simply another manipulative technique which enables people to remain guilt-free while breaking the law, it is necessary to probe deeper into the nature of their enterprise. When we do this, it is clear that the distinctions made by the members of the trade are not simply covers for a money-making exercise. Rather, they reflect what is arguably a genuinely different phenomenon from either normal trade or normal crime.

5. Trade, Money and Motives

> If friends make gifts, gifts make friends. A great proportion of primitive exchange, much more than our own traffic, has as its decisive function this instrumental one; [that] the material flow underwrites or initiates social relations.
>
> *M. Sahlins* (1972:186)

The actual transactions that form hidden-economy trading are characterised by certain features that suggest we are dealing with a distinct phenomenon. In this chapter I describe these features and show how the hidden economy, as exemplified by part-time trading, has its own rules, customs, norms and motives that make it clearly distinguishable from both normal trade and normal crime. What emerges is a picture of an economy in which trade is merely *framed* in economic terms and uses goods, services and money as a medium. In practice, however, the transactions are meaningful because of the social relationships between members of trading networks, rather than because of the monetary benefits they might produce. In this sense, the hidden economy has similarities with the social exchange that occurs in non-industrial societies, in which the material value of items is of secondary importance to their meaning as symbols of relational ties and bonds of friendship.

The Essential Features of Trading

An underlying feature of hidden-economy trading is the preliminary conversations and negotiations which take place over a period of time, long before trading proper occurs. In Chapter Two I discussed how trading networks limit their membership through a series of preliminary, publicly ambiguous rituals designed to test whether a newcomer is suitable to become a trading partner. The rituals are very informal affairs, carried out in such a way that their meaning is limited to those 'in the know'. No similar rituals, relationships or restrictions apply to legitimate trading.

Secondly, all discussion of the actual trading arrangements, such as the price of the goods, their delivery and the methods of payment, takes place openly but carefully. Steve reflected on the fact that, to outsiders, the way some trading went on might seem risky. Showing up on a Sunday morning with a batch of suits could be seen as taking a chance, given the illegality of the enterprise. 'You'd think it would get dangerous,' he said, 'just knocking at the door with them. Freddy's got three kids and the eldest one's eleven and they go round saying, "Daddy's got some suits, Daddy's got some suits". But there's nothing secretive about it. They don't hide behind locked doors—without going out of their way to be daft.' Derek shared the same view. He told me that there was no secrecy or anything like that. 'It's a completely open transaction. You want an item. I can get you that item. Finished. No questions asked.'

The principle that no questions are asked about the origins of cheap goods is a third feature of hidden-economy trading. It contrasts dramatically with legitimate economic activity, where asking as many questions as possible about the goods one intends to buy, is seen as a consumer's right. In part, the 'no questions asked' principle of hidden-economy trading stems from the need to prevent both outsiders from discovering the stolen identity of the goods and insiders from embarrassing knowledge and guilt. In the eighteenth century, the same 'no questions asked' clause was included in advertisements that offered a reward for the return of 'lost' property. The following example was used by Jonathan Wild who, as we have seen, operated a business of dealing in stolen goods, and is taken from the *Daily Courant* of 26 May 1714:

Lost on Friday Evening 19th March last, out of a Compting

House in Derham Court in Great Trinity Lane, near Bread Street, a Wast Book and a Day Book; they are of no use to anyone but the owner, being posted into a Ledger to the Day they were lost. Whoever will bring them to Mr. Jonathan Wild over against Cripplegate Church shall have a Guinea Reward and No Questions asked. (Howson, 1970:66)

In the eighteenth century, the phrase was seen to be little more than a device which protected the trader from the suspicion of instigating the theft. Since then, however, it has become taken for granted in all dealings in cheap goods. Michael, for example, in talking about the origin of some cheap tape-recorders being sold by his friend, said, 'He's pushing them out. But there again, I don't know where he got hold of them. I didn't even ask him.' Likewise Stan spoke of a friend who was selling razor blades, 'How he got them is no one's business, because even I don't know. You don't ask where they came from. You just buy them if you want them.'

As can be seen from Derek's statements, the reason why no questions are asked in hidden-economy trading is to do with neither protection from the law nor protection from the guilt of knowing that the goods are stolen—most members of the trade are so convinced of the justness of their activity that they do not care who knows what they are doing. Instead, it is to do with protecting the trust implicit in a relationship. 'You don't ask a bloke's reasons for flogging something,' said Derek, 'You don't ask "Why are you selling it?" That's an intrusion of their privacy. They've got their reasons. It's up to them.' For this reason, as John the unemployed driver, said, 'You can't ask the bloke whether the stuff's stolen. You can't turn round and say it. If you did, he'd probably start a fight.' Of course, this does not mean that no questions of any kind are asked. In fact, if questions are *not* asked about the size, type, colour and quantity of the goods, for example, as well as their price, then suspicions might be raised about a person's motives.

A fourth characteristic of hidden-economy trading is a general lack of the firmness and precision that is found in commercial dealings. In particular, the price of goods, rather than being fixed in advance, is deliberately vague. A common expression is, 'I can't say how much they'll be till I get them, but they'll be cheap.' Similarly, little is certain about whether or not goods will be obtained at all. Derek's friend, Gerry, delivered cheap coal, bricks and other building materials. On one occasion when Gerry had visited to deliver some coal, Derek asked him about bricks. Gerry replied with the question, 'How many do you want and what colour?' Derek told me that he looked at a few different sorts of bricks and then met Gerry in the pub and said, 'I think I need about a hundred and fifty of such-and-such' and Gerry told him, 'I can't promise anything, but I'll keep my eyes open.' The same vagueness concerning the details of deals was apparent whenever Lucy ordered anything from her warehouse friend. 'I never know whether he'll get what I want,' she said. 'He's never sure. It all depends on what he can get. He's always got to see someone else who's got to see someone else and that's how it goes on.'

Like the 'no questions asked' principle, vagueness about the availability of goods or their price requires a good deal of trust between the parties involved. The buyer has to trust that the price and quality will be satisfactory; the seller must have confidence that the buyer will still want the goods after he has supplied them. No similar trust is necessary in legitimate trading, nor is there any such commitment to completing the transaction.

Another fundamental difference between illegal amateur trading and legitimate economic activity is the different attitudes to time. Normal market exchange puts emphasis on the completion of transactions in the minimum possible time period. It is usually expected that commodities and money will be immediately available. Where deferred payments are part of the contract, the terms of payment are narrowly defined by law and time costs money. Hidden-economy trading, in contrast, is typically permeated with delays, lapses and pauses. Days may pass between the request for goods and the setting up of a deal. It is often weeks before an arrangement is sealed and the goods are delivered. Finally, it might take up to a week before payment is made for the goods received. For example, it took three weeks for Derek's cheap bricks to arrive. When they arrived he did not pay for them immediately but a few days later, when he went to the pub.

Related to the vagueness about the arrangements of a deal and to the delays that are involved, is a sixth feature of hidden-economy trading. This concerns providing *extra* services, such as credit, free delivery and the provision of an excess number of items. A good example of all three of these occurs in the case of the colour televisions distributed by Paul. He not only sold the sets at the ridiculously low price of £60 each, but he took responsibility for destroying the evidence that they were stolen by 'burning all the cases they came in'. In addition, he 'tuned' the sets and provided the cash if someone could not afford the purchase.

> The thing was, they didn't know anybody who could set them up and I had to go round all their houses tuning 'em in ... I managed to move the whole lorry-load, for cash, that night ... See, I had a bit of money with me and I backed people.

The extra services—in the above case, credit and the tuning of the television sets; in the bricks case, free delivery—collectively demonstrate the goodwill and readiness on the part of the seller to 'put himself out' for the buyer. The provision of credit and extras also serves continually to confuse the price and to defer the settlement of the accounts. The most desirable state is never to meet the other person's price exactly. Exchanges are managed so that the accounts are kept unbalanced, with one party in credit and the other in debt. In this way there is always a need to continue with the relationship.

Another significant aspect of hidden-economy trading which, like the provision of credit and extras, confuses the actual material values involved and makes for a continuing trading relationship, is the tendency for payments to be made either wholly or at least partly in kind rather than money. Derek explained how he first learned of the payment system that

84

operated in his particular trading network.

> I was in the pub saying, 'So many coal mines round here. Where can I buy coal?', and someone says, 'Oh, we'll send Gerry round.' So Gerry appeared with two or three hundred-weight of coal and there I was, money in hand, about to pay him and he says, 'Oh, you owe me a pint.' So I said, 'Where does the service end?' He says, 'If you need anything, let me know and I'll see what I can do.'

The expression 'you owe me a pint', or the typical giving and receiving of gifts as part of the transaction, enhances the distinction between market exchange and hidden-economy trading, making it very difficult in the latter case to represent accurately the material value of the goods involved. When Derek's bricks arrived, for example, the cost was obviously more than the pint he had 'paid', but this was only vaguely implied in Gerry's response. Derek told me that Gerry turned up in his coal lorry and the bricks were on the back. 'He took them off, so he says, "Now you owe me a brandy" ... When I went in the pub I put a quid or two behind the bar for him. They chalk it up on his board. See, when he goes in there to buy a drink, it's paid for. It's a way of, you know ... it's like saying "You buy me a drink", but it's a more positive thing than that. It's a good system. It's quite nice, quite pleasant.'

Of course, by-passing payment in money through a kind-payment system like this may also be seen as an effective way of avoiding any illegal involvement in those cases in which the goods are stolen. This is because to deal directly in fixed prices, for money, would make the exchange into a purely commercial transaction, which it is not. The system of payment in kind, nevertheless, has implications for the scale of operation and amount of money that is allowed to be made from such trading. I shall discuss this in the next section.

It is appropriate, too, that 'buying drinks' should be the form of kind-payment system used. Drink is an ideal medium for celebration, as it is taken in a place which is clearly social rather than economic. Social celebration, like the rituals of

85

relationship-forming that mark the boundaries of trading networks, signifies the completion of a deal. Such celebration and ritual would be redundant in typical commercial exchange of Western market economies, though they are typical of barter economies of non-industrial societies.

The 'quid or two behind the bar' is never expected to stay behind the bar, or to be consumed by the recipient alone. Instead, it is to be distributed in drink throughout the group. As Gerald Mars points out in his analysis of drinking among Newfoundland dockers (Mars, 1972), drinking extends social contact beyond the principal trading partners, since it grants the recipient a 'bank of social credit' which he can dispense at his discretion. In doing this, he is enabled to pay back obligations or create new ones, and can thus rise in prestige and esteem. But, more importantly, in converting material resources to social ones through communal drinking, this kind of payment system also reduces the possibility of accumulating capital.

However, a drinks-payment system is only one way that individual members are discouraged from benefiting financially through hidden-economy trading. As I shall show in the next section, a number of other mechanisms are also at work which prevent money from becoming a primary concern.

THE MONEY MOTIVE

On the surface, it would appear that hidden-economy trading, like its professional and legitimate counterparts, is motivated by the pursuit of economic gain; the desire to make a profit and the irresistible lure of money. What Carl Klockars says about his professional fence might seem to apply to everyone who deals in stolen goods. 'Vincent is a businessman. He buys and sells merchandise in order to make a profit. Some of his merchandise is stolen, some of it is not. There is only one advantage to trading in stolen goods; one can buy them cheaper than legitimate goods and thus make a greater profit'

(Klockars, 1974:77). Indeed, Ted Roselius and Douglas Benton argue that 'one must assume that the distribution of stolen property is rather business-like ... and that many patterns of behaviour in distribution are economically motivated (Roselius and Benton, 1973:180).

But it is not only commentators who take this view. Members of trading networks, when asked why they engage in their enterprise, invariably reply in ways which suggest economic motives are involved. They say that they do it 'for the money' on 'for the things they get'. 'If you ask Freddy why he does it,' said Steve, 'he'll talk about the money he gets out of it.' He told me that 'Freddy always claims he's doing allright out of it. He'll say, "I get all this gear cheap, don't I? Look around me. I've got all this stuff that I'd probably have to pay through the nose for, that I probably wouldn't even have."' Stan similarly insisted that he was doing it for the money every time, while Michael and Lucy said they did it for the goods they got for themselves. Michael told me that he always 'made a few bob' on the stuff he dealt in. He always got 'a free packet' for himself. Lucy said she always kept some of the items she was selling. 'That's all I did it for really. Look at those things I got. That Pyrex and the cutlery and those scales. I would never have been able to afford them otherwise.'

Similarly, if we look at the way members of the network talk about how deals operate, the same pattern of explaining motives in economic terms is evident. For example, from the 'exchange rates' discussed among members, it appears that people cannot fail to make money. There is a 'standard rate' of purchase and sale by which goods are bought at one-third of their retail price and sold at a half. 'If Jim comes in and, say, there's a price tag on an item for ten pound, Freddy will buy it at three pound or three pound fifty and flog it for a fiver,' explained Steve. This profit-making rate is the same as that which has been observed in professional fencing (Klockars, 1974:115).

However, close scrutiny of the system shows that hidden-economy pricing is not as clear-cut as it might seem at first. There are various reasons why the 'standard rate' is not maintained. One is that if the goods are of high value, the rate drops. This is because people are not prepared to spend large sums of money on 'cheap' goods. Items which might sell at £300 would be bought at £80 rather than at £100, and might be sold at £120 rather than £150. If there are large quantities of goods, the amount that a trader can get for them is also reduced. As Dave pointed out, traders work a 'wholesale reduction'. A person buying might say, 'If you've got that many I ought to have them a bit cheaper.' 'Dresses at three quid a go are only a dollar each if you've got a lorry-load of them,' said Dave.

In most cases, however, it is unusual for part-time traders to come into contact with highly valuable goods or 'lorry-loads' of them. When these opportunities do arise, traders are often unable to sell the goods. Steve said that rings, for example, were hopeless because people could not assess their value. 'Watches are different because if it's got Omega stamped on it, people will say, "Oh, I know that one." But rings . . . what's a good name for a ring?' The same was true of perfume and porcelain statuettes. But even ordinary goods could prove difficult to sell. Steve illustrated this point with the example of his friend, Syd, a shopkeeper, who bought some cheap salmon.

Take Syd and that salmon . . . He was getting it at half price, so he stood to make half as much again, but very little went through his shop 'cause he couldn't sell most of it. What's the good of twelve cases of salmon to a bloke who only sells two tins a week? He was giving it away to other shopkeepers in the end, just to get rid of it.

Similarly, Margaret, whose husband had been sent to prison for dealing in stolen records, said that he just did not have any contacts to get rid of the stuff. 'It was like a great weight had been lifted off us when he was caught.' Ray told a similar story. 'I've had stuff before that I've "got" myself. I've had it lying there for ages and in the end I've given it away 'cause I couldn't get rid of it.'

Even when large quantities of valuable items can be sold,

members of hidden-economy trading networks do not make money in the sense of making a profit. A classic example of this is the case of Paul's televisions. He spent all afternoon and evening getting rid of every one of a fifteen-ton lorry-load. But he did not make any money on the deal. 'I charged the same price—£60—and never made a penny, not a dime, and I shifted the lot, the whole lorry-load for cash that night.' Nor was this an unusual occurrence. On another occasion Paul was offered some shirts.

I was shown a shirt, a very nice Ben Sherman shirt, and the price was cheap. Of course, I said, 'How many can I have?' They said, 'As many as you want.' If we bought big we could have them very cheap. So we did and we sold them with a bit of a profit. But it turned out that the profit was nothing. It didn't cover the running around we had to do and the inconvenience. You know, you bought four, then brought three back and said, 'Can I change this for another size?', and all this. And then the guy says, 'Do you want any more?' And I say, 'Yes please. I'll come down and pick some up, cash.' And you get down there and you've travelled sixty miles with the cash and the van and he says, 'Sorry, they won't be in till tomorrow.' Allright, so you've got to drive all the way back again. There's your petrol. In the end, that was costing me money.

But it is unusual in hidden-economy trading to deal in such large quantities of goods. In most trading networks much smaller amounts of goods are the norm. Nevertheless, the same feature of a very small profit margin is evident. As Derek says, 'No one really makes any money. Not real money.' He admits that the person who is buying the goods cheap is saving money, but he says that it 'doesn't amount to much'. He points out, 'The bloke who sells it is not actually making anything either. He gets favours in return, more than anything else.' Paul said, 'There just isn't piles of money to be made at it,' and added that he did not think people did it for money anyway. Steve gave a good illustration of non-profit making when talking about the cigarettes he could get cheap: 'I made nothing on them. They were paying 50p for a packet of 60p fags. And I was buying them at 45p. Forget about people making money out of it.' He said there are certain people in any factory who can get cheap stuff: 'It's passed down a line of about twenty people. But they just don't make much money on it. They make coppers most of the time.'

Not only is it the case that part-time trading is unprofitable, but some people admitted that they never, ever, charged more for the goods than they themselves had been charged. Roy sold his paint to 'everyone around the works', as a favour. 'I was selling it for exactly the same price as I was getting it. I wasn't making anything on it. I was doing it as a favour.' Lucy paid half price for everything she got, but 'sold it for the same price'. When I asked why she didn't charge a bit more for everything that she sold, her response was indignant. 'That would have been dishonest!' she exclaimed. The same reluctance to make money is confirmed by Donald Horning's study of pilferers, in which he found that, although 25 per cent of pilferers admitted that they had given goods away, only 6 per cent reported that they had 'sold' pilfered goods. As Horning reports, the taboo against 'selling' pilfered goods was particularly strong. Most workers indicated that selling was morally wrong and 'that the work group would not protect the worker who was removing goods he intended to sell' (Horning, 1970:61).

Why is it, then, that at a theoretical level, that is, when members *talk about* trading, it appears to be an activity in which money can be made and bargains obtained, but at the practical level of operation, this is rarely the outcome? Clearly, part of the reason for this is that members of a trading network usually have a full-time, legitimate job which provides their bread-and-butter wages. They do not *need* to trade in order to live. As Stan said, 'It's just pocket money ... I don't need it.' Also, crucially important is the fact that if real money was made, it would be very difficult to pretend that the activity was honest or to justify it. I will elaborate on this point in Chapter Eight, when discussing how the hidden economy can be self-regulating. However, I believe that a fundamental reason why little personal economic benefit accrues from hidden-economy trading is because the relationships formed between trading partners actually preclude it.

If we look at the *actual*, as opposed to the theoretical or declared, pricing policy in a trading network, we find that it is determined less by market values than by the closeness of the relationship between trading partners. The price charged for cheap goods is hierarchically ranked to reflect the degree of a person's involvement within a trading network and his closeness to the person with whom he is dealing. Generally, the more intimate the friendship between two members, the cheaper the price charged for goods. Close friends and relatives, for example, are often *given* goods and not even charged cost price. 'Freddy never charges the family any extra,' says Steve, 'They get it for the price he paid for it. So he's doing it for nothing a lot of the time.' Steve himself does not charge particular friends at work extra if they are in his trading network. He says, 'You've got to give some to so-and-so at the price you bought them, because whenever he gets something he lets you have it at the price he paid for it.' As Stan observed, 'Somewhere along the line, for some reason, it's become a rule that people never charge their mates as much as what they would someone they don't know.'

When the deal is with someone who is not such a close friend, then some profit is included in the price charged. 'There's not a lot of money,' said Michael, 'it's just a little bit extra.' He explained that in his car wings deal he paid £19 and sold the wings for £20, but 'if the guy wasn't a friend of mine, if it was, say, anybody else, I would possibly have knocked them out for about twenty-five. In that case, it would probably have been worth doing it. But this guy's a friend.' He said it was the same with another friend who sold him Japanese tape-recorders. 'He sells them to me for a fiver and, to anyone else, eight quid.'

However, most of the goods a dealer can get are 'sold' or, more accurately, as Paul says, 'passed on' to friends or relatives in the trading network. It is only those goods remaining that are sold to people who are marginally involved in the network. Some traders, as we saw in Chapter Two, do not deal with outsiders at all. Paul would 'only pass it on to friends', people he was 'fairly close with', and Stan said, 'It's kept largely in the family and friends.' Even where people are marginally involved, despite their very weak relationship with members of the network, they are still not charged as much as the pricing theory would suggest. There are good reasons for this.

As we have already seen, before a person is allowed to become a member of a trading network he has to go through various levels of relationship. While these are partly designed to protect existing members against the possibility that they will be found out, the whole process also serves to select only those newcomers who can be trusted. The discussion of stolen goods as 'cheap goods', in the context of an implicitly meaningful question, such as 'Do *you* want to buy some "cheap" cigarettes?' allows the deal to stop should the newcomer not respond. The assumptions that no questions are asked, and that the activity is practised carefully, both protect the members from being caught. However, should a newcomer successfully accept these taken-for-granted rules and become a potential member of the trading network, he will not only have successfully negotiated the deal, but will also have achieved something else. By following the rules and accepting the members' definitions of the situation, he will have demonstrated that he is one of the group, sharing their attitudes and views about life in general, and the hidden economy in particular. In doing this, he will have expressed, at the very least, a limited friendship. Although he may still be only a distant friend, in the context of the trading network this constitutes more than economic relationship. It is a statement of a person's willingness to take part in the members' rule-governed behaviour, to accept their norms, at least for the time being, and to operate at that level of reciprocity which permeates the more important exchange between friends and relatives. In acknowledgement of all this, the established member is inclined to lower the price to considerably less than it would be if the relationship was founded on purely economic criteria.

The crucial point is that if the buyer had not been a member, had not been accepted as a member in the first place, through the various testing stages of acceptance, then he would not have been offered the goods. In short, then, while framed in terms of economic exchange, the social organisation of the amateur trade precludes the possibility of the members' making any real money. But, at the same time, the passing on of good fortune ensures that members share the small benefits that exist in a way that reflects the closeness of the relationship they have with their fellow traders.

Given that the practical organisation of hidden-economy trading is such that financial benefits are rare, we might wonder what it is about the activity that makes it attractive to its members. We can see clearly that something is very attractive, not only because people repeatedly take part in trading, in spite of its illegality, but also because of the way they describe what they do. Steve described his own trading in cheap goods in almost mystical terms.

When I've had cheap cigarettes I'd be flashing them round the pub, which is the same as you see in factories. Say a bloke comes in with a big stack of fags. Everyone's puffing away for the rest of the day and chucking them around. *It's not just because you got them cheap. There's something special about them. Somewhere along the line they've become special cigarettes.* They're no longer just an average pack of fags that you bought in a sweet shop. There's something different about them. [My emphasis]

The exact nature of this special quality of cheap goods is difficult to determine. As I argue in the next section, it depends, very largely, on the context in which trading takes place. However, we do know that rather than being a function of the material cash value of the goods, the specialness and, for that matter, the attraction, of trading is 'social' in nature. Steve makes this distinction explicitly when he claims:

It's not important in money terms. I believe the money's not the thing. They might say it is in order to justify the risk in terms that everyone can understand, but that's not it. When it comes right down to it nobody *really* makes any money. The rewards are more social than monetary.

93

The attraction of hidden-economy trading lies in the different social rewards it offers. A greater or lesser number of these may be important, depending upon the precise situation in which trading takes place. For example, dealing between friendly neighbours on a housing estate is likely to bring different social rewards from the kind of trading that might take place between workmates in a non-unionised work place such as a restaurant or hotel. As Gerald Mars has wisely observed, in talking about the hidden economy generally, 'Different types of fiddles, emanating from different industries, serve different functions at different times to different people' (Mars, 1976:1). Nevertheless, it is possible to identify two basic categories of social reward that are common to a number of different situations in which trading takes place. These I have termed 'competitive play' and 'reciprocal favours'.

Competitive Play

Hidden-economy trading can be, and usually is, a pleasurable activity, with characteristics and rewards similar to those of play. I take play here to be a temporary departure from reality into a sphere of intense and absorbing fun-activity. Johan Huizinga has captured better than most the essential qualities of play, which, he says, is

> . . . a free activity standing quite consciously outside 'ordinary' life as being 'not serious', but at the same time absorbing the player intensely and utterly. It is an activity connected with no material interest and no profits can be gained by it. It proceeds within its own proper boundaries of time and space according to fixed rules and in an ordinary manner. It promotes the formation of social groupings which tend to surround themselves with secrecy and stress their difference from the common world by disguise or other means. (Huizinger, 1938:32)

94

Overall, hidden-economy trading appears to comprise three kinds of competitive play. First, all the members are playing against the possibility of getting caught. They are at least half aware that they are involved in some kind of questionable activity. As Michael himself admitted, 'They know there is a fiddle somewhere along the line, but they don't know where.' For some, like Margaret, this involves a worrying tension: 'You never know who is going to come knocking on your door, wanting to have a look round.' But for many, like Paul, this tension provides the fun of the game. 'It's a challenge,' he said, 'a bit of excitement. Someone says, "Can you do so-and-so?" and you take the chance. You say, "Yah, sure. O.K."' In the case of the televisions deal there was an ever-present risk of being stopped with the whole lorry-load. As Paul explained, 'Allright, he had the goods-received note and everything's above-board, but what was he doing outside my place, you know, unloading them in the middle of the night?' In this kind of competitive play, trading is not unlike the card game Pontoon, in which the player plays the bank or 'house'.

There is a second and related form of play: To complete a deal is to beat the system and gain control over personal action. This is particularly likely to be a motive where trading occurs in boring, routine jobs in which the workers would otherwise be controlled by the job. Arranging sales outlets and purchasing occasions at work allows people to play the role of entrepreneur and through this they can regain some of the individuality that their job denies them. Trading in any abnormal place, such as work, home or pubs and clubs, is fun anyway, because nearly all trading in our society takes place in the typical settings of shops, stores and warehouses. In these conventional trading situations there is little opportunity for a person to exercise control, because the organisations concerned are usually massive, bureaucratic complexes and always have fixed prices for goods and laws governing their trade. It is for these kinds of reasons that Lucy, for example, finds it more attractive to earn 'a few coppers' selling 'knocked-off dishes' to the 'girls at work', than to stay on and do a little extra overtime.

Sure, I'd get more by doing an hour's overtime, but I don't

want to do that, do I? I see enough of that all day long. It's repetitive and it's boring. I'm tired out doing my work all day. Do you think I'm going to stay here a minute longer than I have to? ... But this isn't the same as work. It's money earned in your own time. You're your own master. No one's telling you what to do. It's the way you want to spend your time.

For the same reasons Syd would get 'slapped on the back' and told what a good bloke he was 'cause he'd got cheap gear'. In both cases, selling and buying had been taken out of their ordinary context into a different world, into a world in which the members could be spontaneously caught up, carried away and engrossed. Like play, trading represents a temporary activity, standing outside normal life, 'satisfying in itself and ending there ... an interlude in our daily lives' (Huizinger, 1938:27).

A third manifestation of competitive play in the hidden economy is the traders' competition with each other. They compete for status and approval in the eyes of the people for whom the goods are obtained. Traders are eager to demonstrate that they will put themselves out far more than the next man. They wish to show that nothing is too much trouble. Many will claim that they are prepared to give the most away. All will give the impression that they are generous to their friends. In doing these things successfully, the dealer is also saying something about his social standing. He is demonstrating that he has a vast hinterland of social relationships, a veritable network of 'people in the know' who have both the influence and the ability literally to 'produce the goods'. Most importantly, he indicates that the network can be put to the service of the person wanting or needing the goods. Maurice's sales representative friend, for example, is held in high esteem:

Terry did it to help friends. He gave me that stuff to sell. He didn't say, 'Give me this amount of money for this amount of stuff.' He just gave it to me and if I sold £100's worth I just gave him £66 and he didn't even bother to check it. He didn't say, 'There's a hundred quid's worth of stuff. Work out how much it is and give me two-thirds back.' He made nothing out of it. What he didn't give to me he shared out among his salesmen. He wasn't interested in the money. He did it to help me out because he knew I was emigrating to Spain. But Terry's that kind of person. He would go into a pub and buy two drinks to everyone else's one. He has to give more than he takes.

Giving goods away for status or simply to demonstrate friend-ship is not unlike the kind of competitive exchange found in the 'potlatch' rituals of some non-industrial societies. The classic example of this kind of giving took place among the Kwakiutl Indians of North America (Codere, 1950). Any claim to a new status, such as a birth, death or marriage, had to be validated through the giving of a potlatch. This was an enormous feast with much pomp and ceremony, during which the person seeking the status confirmation had to give away or destroy property, usually blankets, in very large quantities, showing that he was able to do without it. Often he challenged a competi-tor, who was then obliged to give a return potlatch at which an attempt would be made to match the waste.

In a similar way, members of a trading network issue and take up challenges. Michael's claim that he could get almost anything that was wanted, given time, could be seen as such a challenge. 'I tell you what,' he said, 'you name it and I bet you I can get it. Give me long enough and I bet I can get it for you.' Steve pointed out that there was a lot of this kind of bragging within a network.

There's a lot of boasting goes on around it. It's all surrounded by jokes. Everything they do is very light-hearted. Jim'll knock at the door and say, 'I've been doing a bit of "stock-taking."' You know, big jokes and lots of puns. He's always telling stories about himself and the deals he's made. He'll boast about them. To him it's something to brag about. There's no point in doing it if you can't tell people about it.

The kind of potlatch competition in which goods are given away to gain favour is particularly likely to occur in work

97

situations, where employees, supervisors and managers are ranked differently but work closely together. In the following example, Tom, the assistant manager, competes with the manager for the favour of the staff by giving away the company stock. The assistant manager invariably wins these battles because the manager limits his gifts to 'what the firm can afford':

Tom: Here, stick these in your pocket, but don't let him see 'em. Don't put 'em in that outside pocket. If he asks you where you got 'em you can tell him you got 'em from me.

S.H.: That's very good of you.

Tom: Oh, you better have it, 'cause he won't give it to you. You won't get nothing out of him. He won't give you nothin'. You've seen how he treats me. We're always arguing . . .

Among people who buy goods more often than they sell them, competitive play takes place for the attentions of a dealer. Just as to be let into the trading network in the first place marks a significant shift in status, so being given goods, while others have to pay, is the ultimate demonstration of social standing. Michael recognised the importance of being selected and he rewarded his special customers in a way which reflected this hierarchy. 'Suppose there's a very good customer that comes in, say, every week and you might get to know him ever so well. You know, he might make a cup of tea now and again when he comes in. Well, you kind of chip in on the same block.' Lucy regarded acceptance into her own trading circle very highly and described the accomplishment as showing her 'craft'.

As well as being an exciting game, providing status and prestige, trading is also socially rewarding as a community activity based on a network of relationships in which members do 'favours' for each other.

Reciprocal favours

As I have already pointed out, the bulk of hidden-economy trading takes place between friends, relatives and workmates.

In these circumstances deals often have less to do with the material worth of the goods and more to do with fulfilling the expectations and moral obligations of the friendly relationship. For example, in cases where a person requests cheap goods this request will be fulfilled not to make money, but because the friend wants and has a genuine need for the goods. 'You don't think about what you're going to get out of it,' said Stan.

You don't think, 'Oh, I need something'—say, a new carpet—'right, I'll nick something from work and flog it, then I can buy the carpet.' You don't think about it that way. You just think to yourself, 'Oh, I know someone who wants something like that.' It might be a piece of stone for a fireplace. You think, 'I can get them that', and you sell it to them. Why I do it is because somebody wants it and I can supply it.

Michael had the same idea when he offered to get the car wings. 'I did it 'cause the guy *needed* the wings,' he emphasised. As Derek said, 'On the whole, it's stuff that you have or you can get that somebody else needs.'

The same kind of philosophy prevails when the goods are offered for sale. Purchase is often made not because the buyer stands to make a financial gain, which is more likely to be the case than when someone is selling, but because the seller is a friend. Dick, the voluntary group leader, told me that if one of his mates said, 'I got a couple of pairs of trousers', he would probably buy them to help him out. 'I've been asked if I wanted to buy radios cheap, but I didn't really want to. I just had them to show I was being helpful, trying to be a good mate.' Steve points out that this can actually cost someone a lot of money. He says Freddy buys much more stuff from his friend Jim than he actually wants and he believes that Freddy probably buys and keeps more stuff for himself than he 'knocks out' in the long run. But as Steve says, it is not *just* because the goods are cheap that Freddy cannot resist them. 'He wouldn't want to refuse them because they're good friends. See he's helping him out by buying the stuff.'

Insofar as cheap goods are traded *because* of a relationship between partners in a network, hidden-economy trading can be seen to have parallels with the reciprocal gift giving of non-industrial societies. This is to say that transactions are governed by what Alvin Gouldner has called the 'norm of reciprocity' (Gouldner, 1960:170). According to this norm, when one party gives to another, a moral obligation is generated. The recipient is indebted to the donor and remains so until he returns the gift. The obligation to repay is morally enforced, failure to give and repay being sanctioned by dishonour, shame and guilt. Such reciprocal exchange serves to maintain friendly relationships by ensuring that a 'balance of debt' always exists between exchange partners. As John Davis expresses it, 'The slow, difficult, gradual approach to a matching of benefits, with its attendant intervals of imbalance and trust, is a primary characteristic of reciprocity' (Davis, 1973:164).

We have seen at the beginning of this chapter how trading is characterised by lapses in time between deals and payments, and also how credit is given as a matter of course. But we do not have to tease out these features to demonstrate reciprocal gift giving. Members of hidden-economy trading networks explicitly talk about deals in terms of 'doing favours'. For example, Roy sold his cheap paint 'as a favour to everybody around the works'. Similarly, Paul says he never thinks in terms of how much he can make, but 'If I can do somebody a favour, I will'. This was exactly the case when he took on the television deal. 'You think to yourself, allright, I'll do this guy a favour. He's got a load of it. He can't move it. I'll take some off his hands.' It was the same with Michael. 'You can't expect to make much really because you're kind of doing somebody a favour.'

Derek explained the spirit of trading better than most. He told me that a strong community feeling existed in trading networks. There were those in the community and those outside it. 'If you're in the community,' he said, 'you're prepared to give as much as you can and everybody's giving quite a lot.' When I asked whether this giving was contingent upon knowing that favours will be returned, he said:

Oh, no. There's not that feeling at all. I mean, I've never

100

known it to happen that nobody'll do anything. Not from somebody who's already in the community, you know, really in. It's just accepted. There's no question or doubt whatever. If I go and see old Gerry and ask him a favour, he'll do it for me. And if he came to me, perhaps wanting something, then I'd try and get it. It's the same with any of us here. If you are capable of the job, then you go and do it. And it pays dividends, not personally, but for everyone generally. If you go to a bloke who's done you a favour and say, 'I did this for you. Now you do this for me', which wouldn't happen normally, he'd do it, but not for that reason. He'll do it because you're somebody that'll do jobs for anybody.

Derek also explained that moral sanctions, in terms of decreased social standing, exist. He said that if you are offered something and you turn it down, nobody will think any less of you. 'Not normally, provided you have a good reason.' But he pointed out that if it happens more than once, they'll begin to think, '"You know, all right, he's a nice enough bloke, but he's not really one of us", because they wouldn't do that.'

Derek sees the whole trading network as dominated by this community spirit. 'It may sound odd,' he reflected, 'but it's sort of like a community action group. They wouldn't understand it in these terms; that wouldn't mean anything to them. They just do it. They'll say, "I'll do this for you", or "My brother'll get that for you", this sort of thing.' It was in this way that the trading network, 'worked very well and helped people a lot'. It was for these reasons that he saw trading, although admittedly 'technically illegal', as 'very, very moral—a good thing'. He was certain that those involved 'are not getting anything out of it personally', but felt that, 'they get some satisfaction out of knowing what they're doing'.

We can see, then, that the features of hidden-economy trading are different from those of conventional market trading. While, like market exchange, it is concerned with the movement of goods, any similarity stops there. Unlike market exchange, it is surrounded by important social conventions which suggest a different order of activity. Similarly, it is also different from the conventional stereotype of fencing which, as we have seen in the previous chapter, is presented as a dishonest activity carried out primarily for the pursuit of illegal economic gain. In short, hidden-economy trading has a considerable claim to being regarded as neither normal trade nor normal crime, but as an economy in its own terms. It can be interpreted as an economy operating within a continuum ranging from commercial trade, where exchange is impersonal and contractual, as in supermarket trading, to social transactions, where the exchange is highly personalised, as in the barter or gift exchange of village and rural communities or neighbourhood exchange among urban ghetto groups. To assess whether such claims can be justified, it will be useful to look at the range of exchange systems operating in societies other than our own. This anthropological perspective may also help us to understand the paradoxical situation of members of trading networks, who claim to be motivated by one set of desires but, in practice, seem to find satisfaction in another.

6. Unveiling the Hidden Economy

> ... the differences between primitive and market
> economies do not lie in the presence or absence of
> particular ways of economising. For there are different
> norms of exchange in all societies—all have a mix
> of normative rules combined and patterned in different
> ways.
>
> *John Davis* (1973:172)

We have seen how hidden-economy trading is governed by
rules, customs and traditions that make it very difficult from
conventional 'economic' or market trading. Indeed, the basic
features of trading in cheap goods, as outlined in the previous
chapter, would be termed 'irrational' by economists. At the
same time, a paradox has been revealed. Whereas people belonging to trading networks behave according to the social principles
of reciprocity and community sharing, they nevertheless explain
what they do in terms of rational, market-exchange principles.
They do it 'for the money. Why else?'

To understand this paradox, and also to begin to see why
people not involved in the hidden economy explain such activities
in market-rational terms, it would be helpful to broaden our
analysis. A comparative view shows that similar non-economic
exchange co-exists with other forms of exchange in non-industrial
societies, and reveals that our own society, rather than having
one economy, has a number of component economies. Finally,
taking into account the wide range of activities within the hidden
economy, it can be seen that our society appears to be dominated

103

by its market-rational economy, and we can understand how its sub-economies are seen as functions of the market economy rather than as economies in their own right. This will enable us further to explain the apparently hypocritical morality prevalent in our society, according to which a person can engage in illegal activity and at the same time condemn that behaviour when it is done by others.

MULTI-CENTRIC ECONOMIES

One of the best reviews of comparative systems of exchange is provided not, as might be expected, by an anthropologist, but by an economic historian, Karl Polanyi. In his book *The Great Transformation* (1960), Polanyi shows that rather than having just one economy, most societies have several systems of exchange. They are what he terms 'multi-centric economies', with separate economies for different classes of goods. He argues that the system of market exchange which appears to be of overriding importance in money-based industrial societies like our own is only one of many systems of exchange, and that most non-industrial societies possess at least one, and sometimes two, non-market systems. He identifies these as the *redistributive* and the *reciprocal* spheres of exchange. An example of redistributive exchange can be seen among a Pakistani people, the Swat Pathan (Barth, 1959), whose rice crop is taken to a centre from where it is distributed to the people in the surrounding areas. The best-known example of reciprocal exchange is gift exchange among the Trobriand Islanders of Melanesia, documented by Malinowski (1922). In this case, shell necklaces and armlets are given to neighbouring islanders. Great honour and prestige are attached to particular shells and a giver can create both friendship and social credit by giving them away. At the same time, the gift giving allows trade of material goods to take place and it also minimises political feuding.

In those non-industrial societies which have more than one economy, each system of exchange is seen as distinct and self-contained. It has its own rules, its own morality and, importantly, its own language consisting of words that are appropriate only to exchanges in that specific economy. Because of this, the economies are almost completely separate from one another. For example, a study by R. Salisbury (1962) shows that the New Guinea Siane society has three distinct economies, one for each of three different classes of goods: *valuables*, which are essentially pigs; *luxuries*, such as palm oil and pandanus nuts; and '*things of no account*', comprising mainly vegetable food. The goods which circulate in each of these economies cannot be equated with goods in another and therefore cannot be exchanged. For example, pigs, which are valuables, cannot be exchanged for vegetables (goods of no account) because the two kinds of goods are in separate economies. This can have some interesting side-effects, especially where money is concerned. As a result of technological change, the Siane came into contact with the labour market and acquired cash in the form of pound notes, shillings and coppers. However, these were not treated as money. The Siane identified pound notes as valuables, shillings as luxuries and coppers as 'of no account'. Because of the separation between the economies, a pound note could not be changed into shillings and coppers, neither could a shilling be changed for coppers (Salisbury, 1962:130).

However, isolation between economies in some societies, although fairly complete, is never absolute, and even without a money currency, conversion of goods from one economy to another is possible. A good example of a society with three separate economies but without money is the Tiv, a tribe of northern Nigeria studied by the anthropologist Paul Bohannon (1955). One of the Tiv's economies involved the exchange of subsistence goods, mostly food, household requirements and clothing. Transactions were usually conducted by barter or through gift giving. Shrewdness in negotiating in this economy allowed a person to become affluent. But for prestige he needed to operate in the second economy, concerned with goods and services, including cattle, brass rods, ritual knowledge, magic, medicines and slaves. Brass rods were valuable and were not unlike money, inasmuch as all other commodities in *this* particular economy could be measured in their terms.

The third and most exclusive economy was that comprising

the exchange of people who were not slaves. This usually meant wives. Obtaining a wife among the Tiv could be done in at least two ways, but the preferred way was to exchange a woman who was under a man's control, either as his daughter or ward, for a woman in another family. The greater number of properly exchanged wives, the greater a man's prestige. The problem for a man with no woman to exchange was how to contract a fully legitimate marriage with an exchange wife, when the only currency for a wife was another woman in exchange. It was here that the process of 'conversion' operated through the practice of 'trading up'. By hard effort, a young man first obtained a good reputation and a surplus of subsistence goods. He often had affluence but not influence. He waited until a man of influence wanted subsistence goods. Once he had obtained prestige items such as brass rods, he was well on the way to participation in the top, prestige economy—the acquisition of an exchange wife. Since women could only be exchanged for women, a kind of loan-credit was arranged. The father or guardian of a girl would be 'loaned' in exchange for prestige goods, which indicated the young man's intention to complete the exchange later. When the children were of suitable age, they would be given to the guardian. The loaned wife then became an exchange wife and the exchange was complete.

It needs emphasising that the possibility of conversion between separate economies within a society does not alter the fact that there is no single vocabulary for talking about economies generally. If there are, for example, three separate economies, there are three different corresponding vocabularies. Other studies (for example, Firth, 1965) have described the existence of multiple economies in different non-industrial societies and have also shown that the degree of separation varies between different economies, each possessing its own morality, language and relative prestige rating. Recently, it has been suggested that our own industrial society is also made up of a number of different economies.

Traditionally, it has been thought that almost all buyer–seller relationships in industrial societies are non-personal, especially when they occur in urban settings. According to Simmel (1950), this is to be expected, since such relationships are part of a reserved, matter of fact, non-committal attitude generally adopted by the urban dweller to protect his personal identity from a barrage of psychological stimuli in the metropolitan environment. For others, like Wirth (1938), such impersonal contractual relationships are an inevitable feature of increases in population size, density and heterogeneity. While it is known that intimate social relationships among family, friends and neighbours still exist, it is not generally realised that our whole economy is made up of a number of smaller, personalised economies, whose rules and morals operate differently from those of contractual market exchange.

One such economy occurs where commercial exchange is governed not by the 'calculus of exchange value', but by the 'etiquette of valued exchange' (Faberman and Weinstein, 1970:450). Thus it has been found that some shoppers in an urban setting establish reciprocal friendly relationships with sales and service people in local shops. In a study of thirteen consumer contexts, including grocery, clothing, shoe, drug, hardware and liquor stores, a petrol station, barber shops, doctors, dentists, restaurants and car repair shops, it was found that 23 per cent of buyer–seller interactions were personalised and as many as 11 per cent approached friendship (Faberman and Weinstein, 1970:452). The authors of the study suggest that these relationships may be an attempt by consumers to protect themselves from people on whom they are dependent:

Those who invade the body space to touch, handle, and manipulate us, or who administer esoteric knowledge over which we lack surveillance, have us at their mercy. By defining and acting towards them as friends we attempt to transform a pure exchange of value interaction which leaves us defenceless, into a valued exchange which gives us claim to equality. The expert other must now follow the non-exploitive rules of friendship rather than the exploitive rules of the market. Personalisation may well be an attempt on the part of the client or customer to counteract the superordinate position of the expert by shifting the normative ground of the interaction. (Faberman and Weinstein, 1970:456)

Whether their explanation is correct is irrelevant, since, once the qualitative content of the relationship has changed, for whatever reason, the interaction will go on in ways governed by the rules of friendly reciprocity.

Recognising the existence of personalisation in commercial trading, some companies in the market economy of our society have attempted to use this for their own profit. A classic example is party-selling, as operated by Tupperware. John Davis has described party-selling as 'a combination of sociability and marketing', in which one form of exchange is geared to another (Davis, 1973:167). He sees selling parties as sociable episodes in the ebb and flow of obligations and trust between acquaintances, friends, neighbours and kin, and he points out that just more than half of all housewives go to selling parties and that most of them live on municipal housing estates and have young children. Occasions for formal socialising among these women are not part of their cultural heritage. He points out that:

Parties are commonest in those areas where there are few opportunities for women to work: with young children, without jobs, without the middle-class traditions of coffee mornings, local history groups and political clubs, they are isolated in their houses. I have been told that companies frequently receive letters in which the writer says she has moved to a new neighbourhood or a new town, and knows no one: could the agent please call? (Davis, 1973:170)

At selling parties games are played to create the right mood. One handbook for Tupperware agents suggests that ten minutes should be passed in this way. For example, at a party where the theme of the demonstration was to be the utensils needed to make cakes, the guests competed to write down as many names of cakes as they could. 'Make sure the guests know what the prizes are,' says the handbook, 'and how to use them and let every guest win a prize' (Davis, 1973:169). He concludes by saying that when we examine the performance of our own market institutions, we discover rational manufacturers and profit-motivated entrepreneurs taking into account precisely these obligations to exchange non-commodities in a non-rational way that are observed in primitive societies.

But personalised selling goes beyond making friends with local retailers or organising party selling. It can entail barter between people, in which money plays a far less important part than in the market economy proper.

The British barter economy

In a recent report, Christopher Hudson (1977) documents the existence of a flourishing barter economy in Britain, which he describes as 'the exchange of goods and services between people at a personal level' (Hudson, 1977:17). He says it is not only the rural poor who barter, but everyone, ranging from the person who is good with his hands or has vegetables growing in his back garden to Harley Street doctors. Chickens are being exchanged for lawnmower repairs. Farmers are loaning machinery for grazing rights. Doctors are accepting fresh fruit and vegetables and, says Hudson, a well-known barrister had his appendix removed by a famous surgeon in exchange for a case of whisky. But the British barter economy does not stop at the level of chickens and vegetables. Council houses are frequently exchanged in straight swops, as are holiday homes. Some car dealers have offered to exchange new or used cars for goods and they have, in return, accepted items including porcelain, musical instruments, old cameras and coin collections. As well as local radio swop shows, Hudson says, there is even an organisation called Business Barter Limited, with its headquarters in Yorkshire. Launched in 1975, it runs a directory of members in the north of England who offer services they are prepared to barter. For this they receive a barter cheque which they send to a central clearing house. The person bartering the service is then in credit for the amount of the service he has offered and is entitled to goods to the same value from members in the directory. Perhaps the best example of an economy which is taken to be part of our market economy but which can be shown to be of a different order is the gift economy.

Traditionally, anthropologists have attempted to show that the significance of reciprocal exchange in industrial society has been underestimated. Shurmer (1972:1242) summarises the position, noting that the characteristics of reciprocity apply 'as much to our society as to New Guinea "kula" exchanges or Indian potlatches'. She discusses the giving and returning of coffee mornings, presents, drinks and consumer goods generally in terms of reciprocal gift exchange, and concludes that the reason why all exchanges are not of a contractual kind is that there are 'spheres of exchange', some categories of goods being set aside and seen in non-monetary terms (Shurmer, 1972:1244).

John Davis (1972) takes this argument much further. He criticises the approach that compares total economic systems, saying that we should not talk of one mode of transaction predominating over all others. Instead, he argues that 'the difference between the U.K. whole economy and such economies as the Hausa and Siane are not so much in the "amount of reciprocity", but in the relation of the various sub-systems' (Davis, 1972:409). He considers that the United Kingdom has at least four sub-economies, each distinguishable by the rules which govern transactions within it. The *market economy*, according to Davis, is governed by laws of commercial trading, employment and labour relations. It includes all legal transactions in services and commodities. The *redistributive economy* is governed by laws of taxation, welfare and state expenditure. The *domestic economy* is governed by customs and expectations concerning the relationships between family members. It also includes all productive activities which are not mediated by a market, such as making, mending and food processing. Fourthly, says Davis, there is the *gift economy*, which is governed by rules of reciprocity and includes all those transactions which we call giving a present, making a gift, and so on.

Davis develops the notion of the 'gift economy' which, he says, exists *within* the context of commercial exchange, and which can be studied from market information and records. Drawing largely on consumer research reports concerning the proportion of goods bought by people as gifts, on production figures showing how much these goods cost to produce, and on the retail value of these products to the consumer, he arrives at an estimate for the combined force of gift giving in the United Kingdom of 4.3 per cent of all consumer expenditure. While goods bought as gifts range from greetings cards (100 per cent of sales), toys and games (90 per cent) and automatic tea-making equipment (80 per cent) to jewellery (50 per cent), the largest contribution to expenditure on gift giving was that of beer and spirits. These account for 69 per cent of manufacturers' sales of goods and £542m (at 1973 values) worth of goods—approximately half the total retail value of the gift economy. Davis concludes that the production of gifts is a significant part of all production in the United Kingdom, and argues that there is a primo facie case for arguing that there are transactions in Britain which constitute what may be called 'the gift economy', including goods transferred from the market, from domestic production and 'in some cases from the proceeds of pilfering and theft' (1972:418).

Thus, in the United Kingdom, just as among the Siane and the Tiv, there exists a multiple economy offering, admittedly, easier opportunities for goods to be transferred from one sub-economy to another. However, the failure of people in our society to recognise this has led to their treating the sub-economies as though they operated with the same motives, rules and language as the market economy. In particular, it has resulted in concealment of the activities of fiddling, dealing and stealing, which together make up the *hidden* economy.

THE HIDDEN ECONOMY

Up until now, pilfering, fiddling and dealing have been seen either as part of the market economy or as part of conventional crime. They have been thought to exist in the context of deviance at work and have been included in the same category as production control, output restriction and limitations on innovation. As a whole this deviance, which usually involves collective action by groups of workers, is explained in conventional, self-interested,

111

economic, psychological or political terms. For example, restrictive practices are described as a means of making money, relieving boredom or gaining political control over the productive process to prevent unemployment (Sykes, 1960; Lupton, 1963; Klein, 1964; Dalton, 1964). However, when looked at more closely, these practices can be seen to have motives other than economic ones. They may have aims such as the maintenance of worker solidarity and the development of social relationships in the work place. Particularly interesting here is Donald Roy's study of quota achievement by machine shop workers. Roy (1953) found that striving for and achieving the goal of quota production in a piece-work system carried its own non-economic reward. He said that despite workers' continual reference to its economic benefits, no one *really believed* that he had been making money in the sense of improving his financial status. The rewards were more social than economic.

Similarly, as has been shown in the previous chapter, many of the illegal property transactions which are described as pilfering, fiddling or dealing are not economically motivated, nor are they part of the market economy. Rather, they are part of a separate hidden economy. We have already seen that the characteristics of one aspect of this economy—dealing or part-time trading in cheap goods—has features which are very different from those of its legitimate or illegitimate economic counterparts. We have seen how it is personalised, governed by rules of reciprocity and characterised by a range of social rather than economic satisfactions. In Chapter One I showed how a whole range of illegal activities comprised the hidden economy, and in Chapter Two I described how these were related to each other through trading networks. This analysis can now be broadened to include the hidden economy as a whole.

The hidden economy can be seen as a separate economy existing in two basic forms: as an on-going series of activities traditionally taken to be part of the market and redistributive economies, and, alternatively, as the point at which goods are transferred from the market or redistributive economies into the hidden economy. In other words, pilfering, fiddling and dealing, taken together, are forms of personalised reciprocal exchange or, at the very least, mark the point at which items

112

from market or redistributive economies are dematerialised and the transactions personalised.

The whole hidden economy can be conveniently considered by dividing it into the categories of the economies of which it *appears* to be a part. Thus the market economy can be seen as including production and consumption, while the redistributive economy is made up of taxation and welfare sectors. Taking each of these in turn we can get some idea of the breadth of the hidden economy.

By far the best documented area of hidden-economy trading is that which takes place when goods are being produced or services provided. Indeed, the hidden economy has often been called occupational or employee theft for this reason. But as we shall shortly see, this is really a misnomer arising as a result of concentration on one particular aspect of the hidden economy. Nevertheless, there is a vast range of fiddles that have been seen as part of the market economy. At every stage in the production or delivery of goods and services, a proportion of the activity of employees is really hidden-economy activity. For example, goods are pilfered and fiddled in the course of the transportation of goods through the docks (Mars, 1974), airports (Emerson, 1971; Park, 1973), and on the roads during delivery to factories, shops and offices (Pettigrew, 1977). They are also pilfered during the process of manufacture (Horning, 1970). The area which has received the most attention is the service industries, such as catering (hotels and restaurants (Mars, 1973; Mars and Mitchell, 1976), railway dining cars and cross-channel ferries (Moore, 1976; Needlestone, 1976)) and delivery (milkmen (Bigus, 1972) and bread salesmen (Ditton, 1977c)). But there is also evidence of fiddles in the provision of professional services, such as those by doctors and surgeons (*Evening Standard*, 1976; Pettigrew, 1977), pharmacists (Quinney, 1963) lawyers (Richstein, 1965); managements (Parkin, 1976), executives and administrators (Comer, 1977). Finally, there is a vast range of retail fiddles perpetrated by shop workers, from assistants through to managers (Robin, 1970; England, 1976; Franklin, 1975). Overall, then, we can see that a proportion of what passes for market-economy activity, from raw material, through manufacture, to sale of goods and services, is seen by those

113

involved in it as activity of a different order.

Fiddles by consumers are less well-documented than those by employees, and since customers are not employed by a company (though they may patronise it frequently) customer fiddles are usually seen as theft. A large proportion of all shop thefts (40 per cent, according to current estimates) are said to be accounted for by shoplifting. A classic consumer fiddle is that of price-tag switching (Steiner *et al*, 1976) in which customers swop the price-tag on one item for the tag on a cheaper item. When consumers fiddle certain services, such as telephones or baggage allowances, and bus and train fares it is more difficult to discount this as straightforward theft (Pettigrew, 1977:28).

In the redistributive economy, tax evasion and avoidance are generally the two most prominent forms of hidden-economy activity. Tax evasion consists of taking deliberate action to evade payment by failing to declare some part of income to the Inland Revenue, or it may be a result of ignorance of details of the tax system. Tax avoidance is any legal method of reducing a tax bill, in particular that which takes advantage of a technical loophole in the law (Sandford, 1977). But tax fiddles need not just affect income; they may be worked by businessmen in connection with Value Added Tax (Hopkins, 1977), or by tourists on duty-free allowances. Finally, there are fiddles of social security benefits, known usually as 'abuse' or 'scrounging'. This area has been little studied though it has been much highlighted in the press.

However, it should not be imagined that the hidden economy is a feature only of western capitalist societies. The experience of the Soviet Union has shown that the planned socialist economic system also carries a whole range of semi-legal and illegal markets which one commentator has described as ranging from 'grey' through 'brown' to 'black' (Katsenelinboigen, 1977).

The hidden economies of Eastern Europe

In the U.S.S.R. 'grey markets' exist for consumer goods including apartments, and services such as repairs and private tuition.

114

The illegality of their operation is that the transactions within them are not officially recorded and therefore, go untaxed. Grey markets also operate for producer goods, chiefly materials and spare parts, exchange in this case being by barter. Excess goods, acquired in order to trade successfully in the legitimate economy, are traded for commodities which are temporarily in short supply. Katsenelinboigen illustrates how such a system of semi-legal exchange might operate:

> For example, the chief of the Supply Division at a particular plant might telephone his counterpart at another plant who he knows, and ask him, 'Ivan Petrovich, you wouldn't happen to have such-and-such a shaped metal, say, ten tons of it?' Ivan Petrovich: 'Of course Evsev Abramovich, we can find it for you. But what can you give me in exchange? You wouldn't have, say, ball bearings of such-and-such a diameter?' The answer might be, 'No, I don't, but I'll try to find out from Viktor Iosifovich and then I'll call you back.' And in this manner very long chains of barter arise. ... No use is made of money which might untie the barter relations ... [O]fficials ... accept this procedure of planning because it enables them to obtain personal benefits by a rather safe method, owing to the difficulty of proving corruption. (Katsenelinboigen, 1977:73)

The existence of scarce commodities in the consumer market also gives rise to a 'brown market' in which, for example, saleswomen may tell their friends when a scarce commodity may be arriving. Alternatively, the saleswomen may 'put aside' the item for her friend. Katsenelinboigen says that it is difficult to find sales people making such arrangements with people they do not know, although he points out that the overwhelming majority of sales people participate in this form of selling of scarce commodities:

> Even if a young salesgirl is honest, she is forced to engage in this activity by the department head to whom she must 'kick-back' part of the income and he in his turn, must

115

give a 'kick-back' to the shop director who in turn gives one to the area trade office or to the wholesale base ... and so it goes on until one reaches the very pinnacle of the trade hierarchy. (Katsenelinboigen, 1977:76)

The brown market is also encountered in the production sphere where, because of shortages of spares, managers encourage the illegal production and purchase of stolen spare-parts, which are often made on the basis of personal agreements by workers at the plants. Indeed, Katsenelinboigen points out that the 'black market' in the U.S.S.R. is fed to a certain degree by illegally produced consumer goods made from materials pilfered from state enterprises or stolen from the legitimate trade network. He says that another source of commodities for the Soviet black market is theft from wholesale trade bases or shops that is brought about by 'writing off commodities allegedly spoiled' and 'giving the customer the wrong weight' (Katsenelinboigen, 1977:38).

But the Soviet Union is not alone among eastern European states in experiencing multiple, semi-legal sub-economies. It has recently been claimed that, more blatantly than anywhere in eastern Europe, Poland relies on its secondary economic system. In a report on the country's economic difficulties, Michael Dobbs says that the system of making a lot on the side is booming. All Poles are affected by the dual economy. A peasant sells his meat on the black market, rather than to the state, officials have second jobs as skilled labourers which they do after work, while others, like waiters, may sell their own vodka in state restaurants. Dobbs quotes a Warsaw joke: 'The average Pole earns 4,000 zloties a month, spends 7,000 and saves the rest' (Dobbs, 1977:8).

From these accounts it seems highly likely that multiple economies operate in other eastern European countries and so so in ways similar to their operation in our western society. The crucial issue, however, is not just that there exist a great many different spheres of exchange within any one society, or that the hidden economy can be identified as a distinct economy in its own right; rather, the fundamental problem is to explain how it is that the market economy *appears* to be the only

116

economy in our western society. The explanation for this is to be found in the universal use of market-economy language as though it was a general language applicable to all the different economies in our society.

The Myth of General Language

For many years anthropologists have been aware that talk and description are integrally bound up with particular actions. As we have seen, in many non-industrial societies there is no general language which can be used to talk about different economies. In our society, by contrast, language is not tied to any particular social context. A separate economy, like gift giving for example, is pregnant with the terms of the market economy such as 'reward', 'token', 'bonus', 'windfall', 'legacy', 'subsidy', 'acquisition', 'contribution' and so on. Similarly, the terms of the market economy are used in the hidden economy, such as 'bargains', 'cheap goods', 'perks' and 'incentives'. Using terms from one economy when talking about another confuses the distinctions between economies. Perhaps the greatest contribution to the confusion of economies in our society is the use of a universal measure of valuation, i.e. money.

A money currency, like the Tivs' brass rods or the Siane's 'valuables', permits a material rating of all services, goods or wares, irrespective of their symbolic meaning, and so allows comparative valuation of all items. Money serves an unintended role in providing a 'general' vocabulary, or a nexus of words which governs all forms of transaction, irrespective of context. Such a vocabulary—indeed, such a 'general' language—enables us to talk *about* events in contexts other than those in which they occur. We can 'generalise'. But to generalise in our society means to talk about different subjects, economies or situations in the language of the market economy. It is such generalisation, that masks the difference between different economies. It is in this sense that the hidden economy is truly hidden. Why, then, do the members of the hidden economy talk about their activity in the terms of the market economy?

117

Part of the reason may be self-protection, but this alone is not the complete picture. When fiddling, pilfering or trading occur, the on-going activities are permeated by words and phrases of the market economy, such as 'bargains', 'cheap goods', 'stock-taking', 'turnover', 'orders', 'deliveries' and so on, but these words are used metaphorically. Their genuine meaning is conveyed by the circumstances of the activity and by a meta-communicative language of signs, nods, winks, nudges and hints. Such gestures and cues serve to distance participants in the conversation from the conventional meanings of the words used and to express the specific sense of the occasion. In short, much use is made of gestures which indicate the implicit meaning of the action, the assumptions which members share. Where explicit language is used, phrases like 'doing a favour', 'helping someone out', 'passing things on', 'sharing things out' frequently occur.

In contrast, when the activities of the hidden economy are talked about by the members to outsiders, or by outsiders among themselves, the implicit meaning of the action is missing. The only recourse is to reconstruct the implications of the activity in 'general' language, which, as we have seen, is, in fact, the language of market exchange. In this process all subtleties and distinctions are glossed over and the motives of members are inferred to be those of the market economy: 'profit', 'money', 'goods', 'something for nothing'.

The language of market exchange is, in other words, the socially accepted and only generally available way within our society of talking about, describing and explaining the exchange of goods. But this language, the terms of economic behaviour, has its own set of rules which permit some explanations to be counted as motives and not others. Those which are acceptable explanations in our society are the ones which relate the economic implications of certain kinds of action to the notion of individual property rights (In state capitalist societies these would be public property rights). In other words, what counts as an explanation must be economically rational. For example, this is what Steve meant when he said, 'They say they do it for the money because these are terms which everyone can understand.' Thus the rules of market-exchange language prohibit the consideration

118

of other motives which may be social or founded on the principle of reciprocity. These are represented as 'uncool', 'weak', 'superficial', 'devious', the products of 'rationalisation' and even 'communism'. They are definitely not seen as the real or underlying motive. In summary, when talking about hidden-economy behaviour, people have little alternative but to rely on the socially available verbal resources of a 'general' language that is, in essence, economically rational.

It is for this reason, then, that members of hidden-economy trading explain their actions in terms of economic rationality. When asked, 'Why do you do it?', they reply in economically sensible terms that everyone can understand. They say things like, 'I've always made a few bob on the stuff I've had'; 'I'm doing it for the money every time'; 'All I did it for was to get a few things for myself'; 'I get all this gear cheap, don't I? Look around me. I've got all this stuff that I'd probably have to pay through the nose for, that I probably wouldn't even have.' But, as we have seen, closer examination shows that the meaning of their activity is often anything but economically rational. The hidden economy is truly hidden because it has been linguistically confused. Where this happens, serious misunderstandings can arise which have considerable implications for areas as diverse as morality, industrial relations, social policy and the operation of the law.

One implication of the use of an economically rational explanation is that people can talk about certain categories of events as criminal and even as undesirable, while at the same time they themselves engage in them. In the classic example quoted at the beginning of this book, we saw how people on jury service found nothing inconsistent in convicting someone for shoplifting and then proceeding to fiddle their own jury expenses. Similarly, we have seen throughout how traders may reject goods when they are presented as 'stolen', but accept them if they are said to 'off the back of a lorry'. Contradictions such as these are only made possible by the existence of a transferable language applicable to different economies. By incorporating into their conversation a way of talking about behaviour that transfers it from the criminal category into the ordinary, hidden-economy traders may unwittingly, if conveniently, change

119

the moral implications of their actions. In addition, an action may be seen from different perspectives. Managements may see pilfering and fiddling in terms of the market economy, that is, in terms of economic 'loss'. Conversely, workers may see it in terms of the hidden economy, that is as 'perks'. Whoever is excluded from a particular hidden-economy network may see himself as being denied certain satisfactions and may resort to avenge his exclusion by defining that economy in market terms, thereby invoking all the legal sanctions of property law. In short, people will readily condemn 'all the fiddling that's going on everywhere', but see their own behaviour as 'different'. As Gerald Mars has neatly observed, 'One man's fiddle is another man's perk' (Wallis, 1976). However, there are other serious implications of the dominance of the language of market exchange.

Language and legal control

People involved in the hidden economies of our society may be perfectly happy to explain what they do in market terms. After all, those people who know what it is about and who know the taken-for-granted meaning of fiddling or buying 'cheap' goods will understand the meaning of the meta-communicative nudge and wink. For others, who have no understanding of hidden economy activity, it matters little if they mistakenly take the metaphorical language of market exchange literally. As they are not party to the exchange, it is the only way they will make sense of what goes on and, moreover, it is the only credible 'universal' explanation for behaviour. However, there are certain occasions when the contextual meaning of the language of the hidden economy does need to be explained to those who do not understand it; for example, when someone invokes the machinery of criminal law on the grounds that an offence has been committed. It is under these circumstances that the false 'generality' of language has important consequences.

The handling of law-breakers by courts is accomplished in terms of a legal language. This is a very specific form of highly abstract jargon which masquerades as a refined and objective version of 'general' language. But, as we have seen, general language in the context of the hidden economy is no more than the language of the market economy which has been extended beyond its own boundaries. Legal language, like any other, has its own terminology, but it relies fundamentally on the 'general' language for providing motives. Thus the courts are bound to assess how a 'reasonable' man would behave in a given situation. The motives of a reasonable man are synonymous with those of an economically rational man. Economic rationality is the dominant motive in courts of law.

The legal processing of offenders is done in the court context, in formal, highly ritualised scenarios of account giving (Carlen, 1976). The court bears no relation to the specific context of the action under consideration. It is far removed, for example, from the machine shop or the baker's round, where fiddles or deals may have taken place, and in which the precise meaning of the action was generated. In trying to determine the meaning of a person's action, therefore, the court can only *reconstruct* events from the accounts and descriptions expressed through the 'general' language, which appears to allow a bridging between the two contexts of hidden-economy activity and courtroom ritual. The actions of that economy are translated into the general language by lawyers in the exchanges between counsel for the prosecution and counsel for the defence. But, as we have seen, the only possible motivational structure which 'makes sense' within the 'general' language is that of market exchange. In other words, the 'general' language is 'filled in' with common-sense knowledge of the context of economically rational trade, which is not only inappropriate, but would not even be recognised by its practitioners. In all the ways of talking about events that comprise the everyday activities of the hidden economy, the members never use terms like 'handling stolen goods', 'receiving stolen goods', 'theft by an employee' or 'false accounting', which are the legal terms applied to these activities. As a result, hidden-economy activity, which occurs in its own sphere of exchange, with its own rules, meaning and language, is mystified and transformed in the court setting. It is reconstructed in ways which negate its non-economic or social meaning. For example, we find that the value of goods in the hidden economy

121

is assessed not in terms of their qualitative meaning to those who are involved, but in terms of a market-economy valuation of their price. Nor is the *actual* exchange price seen as significant. Instead, assessment of the seriousness of the 'crime' is likely to be based on the price of the item as if it were part of the market economy. Even in the few cases where a non-economic motive is given credence by the courts, it is implicit that if the practitioner does not confirm their 'commonsense' views, he will be given harsher treatment than might otherwise be the case (Taylor, 1972).

In short, then, the reconstruction of hidden-economy events in the course of court proceedings is based on the erroneous assumption that a general language exists which in some way transcends any particular context and is therefore objective and just. But when it is realised that the general language is little more than the language of another specific context, that of the market economy, we can see what the courts are really doing. They are effectively de-personalising hidden-economy activity and converting its contextual meaning into material values. In doing this, their reliance on a general language ironically reduces their objectivity through its inevitable market-economy bias.

But there is an even more serious indictment of the failure to give legitimacy to other ways of talking, and one that affects relationships outside the courts. I have argued that the language of the market economy, masquerading as a general language, serves to emphasise the dominance of the profit motive in the transactions of the hidden economy and to limit alternative ways of seeing its behaviour. An implication of this is that the people who are given the responsibility for controlling illegal pilferage, fiddling and trading may invoke increasing enforcement of the law and of formal control techniques without being aware of the consequences of their action.

7. Controlling the Hidden Economy

The most salient feature of the entire embezzlement situation is the widespread practice of private justice—private individuals deciding who shall be prosecuted, who condemned, and what, if any sanctions shall be applied ... Certainly it is arguable whether the present situation is not, after all, the best one among practicable alternatives. It is even possible that the described practices and the attitudes they engender, as well as their consequences, are socially desirable, that, in effect, we have an enlightened private individualisation of treatment which avoids the crudities of exposure and punishment and, in sum, is superior to official administration of the criminal law.

Jerome Hall (1952:340–1)

In the previous chapter I argued that the use of a general language makes formal legal methods of controlling the hidden economy unjust. This is because the general language used relies on terms appropriate to the economically rational motives of the market economy. When applied to the largely non-economic behaviour of the hidden economy, these terms make it impossible for courts either to understand properly or to represent fairly the activity in question. However, while such linguistic confusion presents a major problem in the pursuit of justice during criminal processing, it is not yet a major difficulty for the hidden economy. This is because the typical, and indeed traditional, form of control for pilfering, fiddling, dealing and other hidden-economy activity is private justice, carried out by the organisation in which the activity has taken place.

PRIVATE JUSTICE

Traditionally, the hidden economy has been characterised by a lack of interference from outside enforcement agencies such as the police and the courts. This is due partly to the involvement in offences and legal infractions of victims who do not realise they have lost property. Company owners and managers often remain ignorant of fiddling and pilfering, especially if they have been used to treating such losses as 'waste' or a result of poor stock control. Similarly, shopkeepers and wholesale outlets may be unaware of shoplifting or pilfering by sales staff if they have always regarded such losses as 'shrinkage'. The evidence for apprehension rates in the work force suggest that no more than 0.5 per cent of employees are caught for property offences against their employer (Robin, 1970:123). Similarly, J. P. Martin (1962) found that while 82 per cent of the large firms in his study and 56 per cent of the small firms admitted to thefts by employees, in large firms the official apprehension rate was one in 269 of the workforce (0.4 per cent), while for small firms it was one in seventy-three (1.4 per cent).

If we compare these rates with the evidence of studies looking at the percentage of employees who actually *admit* to stealing, the picture is very different. Lawrence Zeitlin (1971:24), for example, suggests that in retail establishments three-quarters of all employees are stealing, while David Cort (1959:341) discovered that 75 per cent of chain-store employees steal. Similarly, Donald Laird (1950:211) described an American drug manufacturing company that used lie detector tests on its employees and found that, in all, 76 per cent of them admitted committing petty thefts. Finally, Horning (1970:60) found that 91 per cent of his sample of industrial workers reported pilfering goods from their factory. Overall, then, it would seem that the number of employees engaged in hidden-economy activities is about one hundred times as great as the number caught. Moreover, this does not include the trading in pilfered and fiddled goods that goes on after these people leave their offices, shops and factories which, Horning found, was done by one-quarter of these who pilfered (Horning, 1970:61).

But undiscovered offences are merely part of the explanation for a tradition of limited official legal control. Even when hidden economy crimes are discovered, they are rarely reported to the police. For example, William Belson, in a study of the public's relationship with the police, found that there was a general reluctance to contact the police when people knew of someone trading in stolen goods. Whereas 99 per cent of his sample said they would contact the police if their home was burgled, only 33 per cent of them said they would do so if they 'knew someone was selling something that had been pinched' (Belson, 1975:45). Perhaps it is more surprising to find that when the victim is a company the offence is still not reported to the police.

J. P. Martin, in his study of English employee theft, found that in large firms the police were contacted in only 31 per cent of cases and in small firms this rate was a mere 21 per cent (Martin, 1962:90). In addition, Martin found that prosecution for discovered employee property theft was considerably lower than for other crimes. He found that larger firms in his sample prosecuted in only 41 per cent of the cases and smaller firms in only 24 per cent (Martin, 1962:86). Gerald Robin, in his study of the way employee theft is dealt with in America, produced similar findings to those of the English study. Basing his study on the occupational crimes committed in three large, independent department store companies, he found that, overall, only 17 per cent of the 1,681 apprehended employees were eventually prosecuted. He points to considerable variation in attitude towards prosecution among the different companies. Only 2 per cent were prosecuted in one company and 8 per cent in another, but 34 per cent were prosecuted in a third. Furthermore, it is interesting that of all those prosecuted, 99 per cent were convicted but only 5 per cent were given penal sentences. Finally, Anthony Christopher of the Inland Revenue Staff Association estimated that tax evasion in 1970 amounted to as much as £500m. However, in 1972, there were only 17 prosecutions for false income tax returns, although 80,000 cases were 'settled' without prosecution.

The policy of companies and organisations in dealing with caught offenders is fairly consistent. On the whole, as Robin found, apprehension for employee crime 'resulted in immediate discharge, but rarely in prosecution' (Robin, 1970:121). As Jason Ditton crisply commented, '"caught" for the employee thief rarely means "court"' (Ditton, 1977c:181). But whether or not an employee is sacked depends upon a number of factors. Ditton showed that if an offence is discovered while it is in progress, it is often summarily dealt with and laughed off. Only where the offence is identified as theft may it result in a warning of dismissal. An example of this occurred when one of Ditton's bread salesmen had been brought before the managing director for reported theft and told, 'If your name is mentioned again, you're going to take a long walk up the road' (Ditton, 1977c:183).

Most commentators agree that for an employer to take the matter as far as dismissal, or further, depends very largely upon whether the offence is actually regarded as theft, and this is often determined by the quantity or value of the goods stolen. For example, a worker interviewed by Horning told him what happened if someone was caught pilfering on the plant. '. . . It depends upon the item. You're fired if it's large—warned if it's small. Their policy seems to point to large quantity or high value. If you take often and are caught, you're fired. If you do it occasionally then you are just warned' (Horning, 1970:61). As Martin showed, half the firms in his sample stated that theft only began when the goods were worth £5 or more. Robin similarly found that, at the time of his study, the critical value for a crime to be seen as a theft and worthy of prosecution was $100. Only 19 per cent of those who stole less than $100 were prosecuted, compared with 57 per cent of those who stole more (Robin, 1970:128). More recently it has been suggested that a universal scale of values should be adopted by all businesses, with different values of property stolen representing different degrees of legal action (Moore, 1975:126).

As we have seen, the preferred course of action taken by employers in cases of discovered theft is to settle the matter 'privately'. Martin found that on almost 70 per cent of occasions when an employer failed to report the offence to an outside agency, he was attempting to minimise the unpleasantness for both himself and his employees. He argues that, in general, the employers' control policy 'may be described as a mixture of humanity and expediency' (Martin, 1962:104). To see exactly what this means we must look at the social, structural and commercial benefits for employers in dealing with offences themselves.

Historically, the system of private justice can be traced back to the servant–master relationship between employer and employee—employee theft originally being called 'larceny by servant'. The relationship of an employer with his employees was often close, if not intimate, and the dependency of an employee on his employer gave the latter considerable control, in the same way that parents exercise control over their children. At the same time, this structural dependence engendered a certain degree of humanity on the part of the employer. Even in small firms today, of which there are 800,000 in Britain, employers may have a personal feeling for their employees. This attachment may range from friendship, as a result of knowing the employees' families, to a kind of protective attitude as a result of an appreciation of their workers' services. Employers, therefore, may be sincerely sorry for the person who has, as they see it, 'succumbed to temptation', and consequently may feel that dismissal is sufficient, or even too harsh a punishment, in itself. The 'soft' policy is particularly likely to be implemented when the offender's work record is good. Additionally, if the relationship between the employer and employee is close, it might be especially difficult for the former to see the latter as a 'real' criminal (Hall, 1952:318). Factors like these could account for the lower reporting and prosecution rates of small companies as compared with large ones (Martin, 1962). However, too much significance should not be attached to these humanitarian or paternal attitudes, since it is just as easy to argue that they

127

could lead a company to invoke punitive measures against the employee, beyond loss of employment, on the indignant grounds that the worker has 'bitten the hand that feeds him' (Robin, 1970:122).

More cynical commentators account for the general preference of private rather than public justice in terms of good commercial business sense. Most recognise that there are three basic reasons why employers opt for imposing their own sanctions. First, there is the employer's fear of bad publicity. If the case comes to court and gets press coverage, the company may be thought to attract bad staff, suggesting in turn that their work may be careless and the company's products of poor quality. In addition, the employee may give some sensational information about the company, like 'everyone in there is at it', or 'the company is just as bad'. Finally, the employer may fear criticism from the court, which may accuse him of poor supervision or inadequate security precautions, and of tempting the workers to commit their crime. Taken together, the risks of adverse publicity from a court case are overwhelmingly high.

A second reason why employers may prefer to take a soft line, either in not pressing for prosecution, or in refraining from giving dismissed employees bad references which would label them as dishonest, is the risk of reprisals. A company might, for instance, be counter-charged over wrongful dismissal, false arrest, malicious prosecution or victimisation. All of these are especially likely where workers are unionised.

Third, and most important, however, are the numerous economic costs which inhibit an employer's action. Apart from the major costs of loss of production through strike action, the range of other costs might include those of prosecution, investigation of the theft, the assembling of evidence, inconvenience and time spent in going to court. Such costs may be especially inhibiting when the amount stolen is small. As Jerome Hall says, the possibility of obtaining economic restitution for the loss in return for not prosecuting is so high that it reduces the crime to a private transaction, 'the defalcation being viewed as damage that can be fully repaired by the payment of a certain sum of money—like breach of contract' (Hall, 1952:311). He says that restitution pervades and defines the entire meaning of this kind of offence. For Ditton, the position is easily summarised.

> Irrespective of the high rate of successful prosecutions which employers are able to secure against their employee offenders, taking people to court is a costly and time consuming venture. The usual managerial folk-wisdom quite accurately reflects this: the normal conclusion is that non-moral tolerance of employee theft is *cheaper* than preventing it in the first place or than attempting to recover the loss through the courts. Whilst there may be specific cases where court action might secure restitution, in general, and as far as employers are concerned, there is no room for civic sentimentality in business. (Ditton, 1977d:7)

In many ways, then, this form of private justice may appear to be an enlightened form of treatment 'superior to the official administration of the criminal law'. It takes into account the background of the person caught fiddling. He is not forced through a public degradation ceremony based on a principle of moral justice. The job he has may be lost, but at least he is not stigmatised by being given a criminal record. Often reference to the offence is also absent from his employment card. From the employee's point of view, settling the matter privately may be taken as management tolerance, company leniency and, in the main, a soft option.

At the same time, the employer is able to make good his economic loss. His action has considerable deterrent impact *within* the company, while avoiding adverse publicity that would accompany a public trial. Crucially important, he can avoid any further investment of time and money in a deviation from his business activities. However, whereas it may seem to be in the mutual interest of both parties to negotiate a private settlement, there are severe problems which make this particular form of private justice an undesirable method of control.

PROBLEMS WITH PRIVATE JUSTICE

The problems of private, paternal, commercial control are best considered in two separate groups. The first comprises all those abuses of justice that are likely to occur as a result of the absence of both democracy and public accountability, the product of a situation in which the victim, prosecution, judge and jury are one and the same person. The second group of difficulties includes those arising from the paradoxical situation where emphasis is placed on hidden-economy crime as a mechanism for controlling labour relations and wages.

Abuses of justice

The injustices of private settlements between an employer and employee begin at the level of discovery. Companies may do without systematic security precautions and equipment on the grounds that these can prove very expensive. Ray Palmer, for example, quotes the director of an engineering company who said, 'Security can entail so much paper work that you reach the ridiculous situation of it becoming more expensive to stop the pilfering rather than to let it continue' (Palmer, 1973:21). Instead, the company may opt for arbitrary spot checks or may even rely on employee crimes 'coming to light' sooner or later. In such a situation workers may feel that their particular offences are being arbitrarily 'discovered'. In the same way, the decision to take action against an employee may vary within a company, depending on the employer's *personal* knowledge of, or dislike for, the person concerned. For example, one employer told Martin that deciding whether or not an action was pilfering or theft depends on the person. 'If you know a chap is a bit of a rogue, it is different from an honest man' (Martin, 1962:117).

Equally unjust is the situation where one company's policy differs from another with regard to the level of hidden-economy activity tolerated. One firm may deem the activity to be perks if the amount stolen is less than a certain figure. The same amount in another company might warrant dismissal and prosecution. Inconsistencies like this are not, however, peculiar to the private settlement of offences, as examples are just as common

130

in the public administration of justice. With shoplifting cases, for example, some magistrates impose the maximum fine of £400, others fine the offender £10 and some let offenders off even more lightly. In a study of English courts it was found that there were 'considerable differences . . . between the sentencing policies of small courts with low case-loads, mostly held in rural areas, and large courts with heavy case-loads, sitting in metropolitan areas' (Hall Williams, 1965:23). Overall, the evidence shows that 'individual differences of approach between judges are the main reason for the disparities in sentencing' (Hood and Sparks, 1970:152). More recently it has been shown that sentencing can be affected by the pressure barristers put on defendants to plead guilty to crimes of which they are innocent. Reportedly, 70 per cent of a sample of defendants changed their pleas from innocent to guilty as a result of barristers' pressure, when they stood a fair chance of being acquitted (Baldwin and McConnville, 1977).

Finally, compared with the amount of evidence required to obtain a conviction in the courts, private commercial justice can operate with minimal evidence. As Martin (1962:75) has pointed out, this form of justice creates the possibility that employees may suffer sanctions, or even be sacked, for offences which in law would only lead to their being treated as suspects. In short, the abuse to which the traditional private system of control is vulnerable is in direct contrast to the principles of formal justice. This insight has been brilliantly captured by Jason Ditton, who concludes a comment on commercial social control:

If legal control may be characterised as having a moral basis, guilt-orientation, formally bureaucratic style, technical-judicial decision making and public hearings; then in contrast, commercial social control has a calculative basis, a profit orientation, an eclectic ad hocness in the procedures by which it comes to decisions, a 'rough' sense of justice, with mock 'trials' held in private. Not to put too fine a point on it, commercial social control is everything that legal social control should *not* be. (Ditton, 1977d:8)

The real irony of the traditional method of controlling the hidden economy is that many employers see its existence as functionally beneficial rather than disadvantageous. Rather than desiring to control it, they turn it to good commercial use. Essentially, their tolerance of the hidden economy is based on their existing control of it and their freedom 'arbitrarily' to choose what to allow and what to enforce. Dalton (1964) was one of the first to suggest some of the ways in which institutionalised pilferage and fiddling in the form of perks may be used by employers as a reward. He identified a number of ways, for example, in which employers can reward their managers for work that is 'beyond the call of duty'. He shows how non-formalised rewards may be offered in place of increases in salary and promotion. He says that such rewards may be used as a bonus for unpleasant work; to off-set loss of status; as a means of sealing an agreement; and as an acknowledgement of personal effort, achievement or sacrifice. The rewards themselves may amount to no more than *allowing* certain hidden-economy activities to continue or making new fiddling opportunities available, as perks.

An employer may also give perks and allow fiddles to operate in order to overcome various external constraints, such as government pay policies which inhibit official pay rises, or to maintain differentials and incentives where these have been either abolished or eaten away by inflation (McHugh, 1977). However, as Gerald Mars pointed out in outlining the range of 'functions' served by institutionalised fiddles and pilferage: 'This kind of fiddle provides an extra control to management and, of course, the reverse applies; the withdrawal of such a fiddle can also be applied as a control and offered as a penalty of humiliation' (Mars, 1976:3).

Mars says that companies may well allow hidden-economy activity in order to provide an element of fun and pseudo-control in otherwise boring, routine, over-structured jobs. As well as relieving employers of the responsibility of making such jobs more interesting by devolving some of the real control over work situations, hidden-economy activity may also foster a spirit of individualism which prevents unionisation of the work force. In this way, says Mars, the employer can avert collective action and strikes. However, Mars points to a far more serious problem: institutionalised fiddling and pilfering is sometimes first allowed to be taken for granted, as providing both economic and social satisfactions, but is later used as a potent weapon for controlling a labour force by *preventing* unionisation. A good illustration of this is to be found in the catering industry.

According to the National Economic Development Office estimates, only 13 per cent of the workers in the catering industry are unionised, despite the fact that its workers are some of the lowest paid and least secure in their jobs. Mars and Mitchell (1977) explain this in terms of payment by the fiddle. They argue that managements in the catering industry have been reluctant to allow unions into the industry because a move to collective, rather than individual, contract making would limit their flexibility over manpower, which is necessary because of the erratic nature of their catering market. Mars and Mitchell say that catering managements have turned the situation to their advantage by manipulating the opportunities for hidden-economy activity in favour of the company's core staff. 'A man making extra untaxed income, that he feels is individually allocated to him, is unlikely to respond to calls by a union official to join in collective action' (Mars and Mitchell, 1977:9). They say this reluctance is particularly likely if he suspects that his industrial contract benefits will decrease in the process and when he knows that any benefits gained through collective action will be taxed at what are now seen as high marginal rates. To seal the issue of unionisation, catering managements are able to make a scapegoat of any emergent union organiser as a pilferer, or to dismiss him on the grounds that he has been caught fiddling, a charge which is nearly always sustainable.

The overwhelming possibilities for abuse and exploitation indicate that the existing private methods are inappropriate as a system of social control and justice. While overcoming the crudities of stigmatisation for offences that are common in the official administration of criminal law and by-passing its inherent linguistic biases, the traditional approach is open to, and suffers from,

133

its own internal disadvantages. The indications are that there exist considerable pressures for change.

THE PRESSURE FOR CHANGE

The hidden economy does not exist in a vacuum. It is influenced by wider events. Not for nothing does the Outer Circle Policy Unit have a working party studying the hidden economy. And there is far more to the attention recently devoted by the media to fiddling than a concern for the moral fibre of the nation. As we saw in the previous chapter, even though it is a different kind of activity, the hidden economy is overwhelmingly and importantly influenced by the language of the market economy. 'Separate' does not mean 'isolated', and inevitably the hidden economy is affected by social, economic and political developments. Notably these developments have an effect at the point where interests conflict. Thus, it is in controlling the hidden economy, when attempts are made to assess non-economic satisfactions in material terms, that the pressure for change is of greatest significance. The most important of these pressures is the recent super-inflation of the market economy and the growth of state intervention in managing it.

Market economy, inflation and state control

During periods of rapid inflation, prices are high and money is scarce. Market economies experience a record number of bankruptcies and some major public companies collapse. Most managements are concerned with the survival of their business rather than extra profit. At such a time pressure is likely to force people to find new ways of saving. In these circumstances, public attention is focused on 'wastage', 'loss' and 'shrinkage'. Between 1973 and 1976, when inflation in Britain peaked at about 30 per cent per year, following an energy shortage and taxation at 35 per cent, it was perhaps no coincidence that

134

workers on the fiddle became front page headlines. Commentators urged British industry to look into its losses from thefts. One commentator said, 'At a time of crippling inflation, the urgency of a review by all concerns, whether large or small, of all their operations where fiddling might be prevalent, in order to cut losses which must be reflected in higher prices, cannot be too strongly stressed' (Traini, 1974:189). It has been pointed out that whereas controlling inflation is a priority, a major contribution to inflation is 'wastage':

> ... most people seem blissfully unaware that the prices of the goods they buy are affected not only by the balance between wages, production costs and profits and by industrial efficiency in general, but also by the depletion of raw materials, components, finished commodities of all kinds—and indeed paid for working time—as a result of dishonesty, carelessness and waste. (*Security Gazette*, 1974a:365)

Similarly, an article in *The Guardian* was one of many which urged businessmen to reconsider their losses in terms of theft. 'Before retailers ask the customers to help with declining standards of honesty, they could talk honestly to one another about theft instead of "shrinkage" and "shortages" and what theft is costing them' (Wainwright, 1976:18). Such redefining of the previously ambiguous term perks as theft leads to pressure on employers to adopt formal control methods and to a more active prosecution policy.

However, two years of successful government wage restraint in 1975 and 1976 under the 'social contract' has delayed the rate at which formal regulation policies have been adopted. This has occurred partly as a result of the usefulness of the hidden economy in maintaining the wage-restraint policy. As we have seen, allowing fiddling and pilfering to continue compensates for diminishing differentials under inflation, and also for a lack of collective activity as a result of the absence of free collective bargaining.

Whatever the outcome in the post-inflationary economic situation, all the indicators point to some formal control over hidden-economy activity. In the unlikely event that wage restraint continues after the relaxation of the pay policy, then pressure for this control may become particularly vigorous in non-unionised areas such as the service industry. As Peter Mitchell (1976) has pointed out, this may be necessary in return for the continued acceptance of an incomes policy by trade union bureaucracies. The unions could benefit from expansion since unionisation would be the only available means by which workers could retain both the economic and the social rewards of their jobs.

The more likely event of a wages explosion may have some dramatic implications for the introduction of formal control policies. A breakdown of the 'social contract' between government and unions through excessive wage rises, and determination by the government further to reduce or prevent inflation, could lead to a special situation of control. With the unions demanding free wage negotiations, government and management may crack down on the only area of control they have left: the hidden economy. This situation may inevitably lead to confrontation, but that would depend upon timing. It would also depend upon how far the unions saw the formal control of fiddling as an exchange for allowing relatively unbridled wage rises and, indeed, how far wage rises alone could compensate for what the hidden economy provides. Whatever the direction of the post-inflationary industrial relations struggle, there are several additional pressures which might also work in support of the introduction of formal control of the hidden economy.

Other pressures

A forceful pressure to effect change in the control policy of companies is that of organisational size. We have seen from Martin's (1962) study how the rate of both reporting and prosecution of employees suspected of theft varied between small companies and large ones. For small firms these rates were 21 per cent and 24 per cent respectively, whereas for large firms they were 31 and 41 per cent. This variation was accounted for in terms of the relatively close personal relationships of workers and employers in the small companies and the greater

136

ability of large companies to afford and benefit from public prosecution. Therefore, a general decline in the number of small companies and an increase in the number of large ones would mean an overall increase in the use of formal public controls.

Pressure for this kind of control is also a product of the general trend towards formalised work relations. In the years since the passing of the Contracts of Employment Act in 1963, a massive amount of labour relations legislation has been instigated by government. Eight key Acts in this field include: the Employment Protection Act (1975); the Sex Discrimination Act (1974); the Health and Safety at Work Act (1974); the Trade Union and Labour Relations Act (1974): the Equal Pay Act (1970); the Redundancy Payments Act; and the Race Relations Act. One commentator has said that the formalisation of labour relations has now reached the point where many of the country's 800,000 small firms are becoming so weighed down that they are having difficulty in understanding or in implementing the various Acts. In this context it is likely that the formalised control of hidden-economy activity is not too far away. But even these present Acts affect the traditional 'private' control of the hidden economy. In particular, the Employment Protection Act makes sacking on the spot virtually a thing of the past. It allows people who feel they have been unfairly dismissed to apply to a tribunal for reinstatement or compensation. Indeed, companies are already increasingly being challenged in dismissal cases. In 1971 there were 9,500 cases in which an employee was claiming reinstatement for unfair dismissal. By 1976 this figure had risen to 43,000 (Fryer, 1977:53).

Another important development which will tend to influence the rate at which formal controls of the hidden economy are adopted is the introduction of industrial democracy following the Bullock Committee's Report (1977). Bullock proposes that workers should gain greater control of a company by joining the boards of directors. If this recommendation is put into effect, it will give workers the power and the knowledge to affect company policy in crucial areas, such as production and marketing. It is argued that existing collective bargaining has been ineffective, since it has specifically neglected these bases of decision making. Bullock's plan may provide the non-monetary satisfaction that is currently being obtained from hidden-economy activity and so make this redundant. The hidden economy might be felt to run counter to the newly shared responsibility of making a profit. Indeed, it would be interesting to know whether hidden-economy activity goes on in workers' co-operatives, but so far this has not been researched. However, the hypothesis that control over the work situation would actually decrease the amount of hidden-economy activity is not supported by the fact that top management, who report a high degree of satisfaction with their jobs (*Which?*, 1977), are just as fiddle-prone as anyone else (Comer, 1977). What is more likely is that the kind of fiddles done would change.

The most important single pressure for the introduction of formal control policy is the growth of the private security industry. Nor is this surprising, since it is private security companies that stand to gain most from such changes.

THE PRIVATE SECURITY SOLUTION

Private law enforcement for industry is not new. Private forces grew up parallel with the civil police and originally existed in the docks and on the railways from the mid-nineteenth century. Since then they have spread to airports, markets and atomic energy plants. Eighteen separate forces currently exist, each responsible to a separate public body. They include the British Transport Police, the British Airports Police and the U.K. Atomic Energy Constabulary. However, the power and effectiveness of these forces is strictly limited by their size and the policies of their governing authorities. For example, the British Airports Police is only staffed by about twenty detectives and the British Airports Authority has a policy of keeping the airports open, no matter what the cost.

On the various occasions when the civil police have been brought in to strengthen the control of industrial theft, the results have been disastrous. For example, when a Metropolitan Police squad was called in to help airport police and arrested two baggage loaders under suspicion of pilferage, there followed an immediate strike by fellow ground staff, who held a protest meeting. A union shop-steward urged fellow workers at the airport to 'have a go' at the police. The meeting condemned the police as 'the Gestapo' and the officers in the arrests were described as 'a snatch squad' (Park, 1973:7). Speaking on behalf of his union, the shop-steward said that in future baggage handlers would be armed with pick-axe handles to deal with any plain-clothes policemen suspected of snooping on ground staff. Similar incidents have occurred in the docks.

Even if the civil police could be eased into a role of industrial and commercial law enforcement, with the prior agreement of all concerned, there would still be the economic difficulty. With reduced public spending, a recruitment problem resulting in undermanning, wider duties and a rising official crime rate, the civil police would not be capable of assuming this wide-ranging new responsibility. Therefore, in a context of increasing public awareness of hidden-economy activity and acknowledgement of the economic and political impracticality of using conventional civil police, governments have implicitly backed the commercial-ised private security industry as the solution to industry's 'crime' control problem. Indeed, the most recent United Nations (U.N.) Congress on the Prevention of Crime and the Treatment of Offenders, in its report *Crime Prevention and Control* said:

Property crime has now reached such alarming proportions in many regions that some commercial institutions have found it necessary to seek protection from sources other than the regular police in order to guard their buildings and facilities on a 24 hour basis. The regular police ... could not be expected to provide such protection to the exclusion of the needs of the community as a whole, and as a consequence, private security companies fill this need. (Stead, 1975:381)

The same Congress discussed the emerging roles of the police and other law-enforcement agencies. It was argued that the major functions of private security were to prevent, detect and report to the police criminal acts concerning private property, to protect against fire and to control access to private property in accordance with the instructions of the owner. These functions were deemed to be completely separate from those of the public police, whose responsibility was to maintain public order, enforce laws, investigate crimes and apprehend offenders.

The U.N. Congress stressed the rapid growth of private security organisations world-wide and pointed out that in some companies the number of security personnel was so great as to exceed the number employed by the civil police. In Britain, for example, although it did not get fully off the ground until the formation of Securicor in 1947, by the 1960s the private security industry had become well established. In 1967 eight private commercial security organisations formed the British Security Industry Association (B.S.I.A.). This now has around sixty members, who transact about 90 per cent of all security business between them (Wright, 1975:274). The total manpower of the private security industry is currently well over 100,000 and exceeds the entire civil police force (Bowden, 1977:350).

The increase in 'loss' control in the retail industry shows how the commercialised private security industry is moving in to control hidden-economy activity as a result of government support. It also indicates the direction in which the whole hidden-economy law enforcement situation is likely to move. In 1973 the Home Office working party report, *Shoplifting and Thefts by Shop Staff*, was published. The report says that there is no doubt whatever the main solution to the problem of minimising losses of stock and money lies with management. It discusses the role of the security industry and says this is a valuable aid to the retail trader in prevention and detection of thefts. The working party is emphatic in its view that all detected cases of stealing should be reported to the police, and that cost-effectiveness is not the only criterion by which crime prevention measures should be judged. The reluctance to report staff is difficult to understand, says the report, as the police are in a better position than the retailer to judge whether or not to prosecute.

In their anxiety to stem what they now see as increasing losses from 'theft', a view enhanced by government pressure to do something, retailers have now joined forces with that 'valuable aid', the security industry. In 1975 retailers and security companies got together to form the first voluntary national

140

crime prevention organisation, the Association for the Prevention of Theft in Shops, which aims to persuade the public, magistrates, parents, teachers and customers that they must do something to control shop theft. One part of its activities comprises publicising the estimated figures of goods lost through shop theft, which it currently puts at £635m a year. Another is to make the industry 'risk-management' conscious and familiar with loss prevention and loss-analysis techniques.

What has happened in the retail industry is happening in other areas of industry at a much slower rate. No doubt if the Home Office's five-year study on industrial losses had been reported instead of being abandoned after six years of confusion, the rest of industry would also have moved to an embrace with the private security industry. At present, the security industry is having to rely on its own publicity to stimulate an interest in risk-management and to translate perks and fiddles into theft loss. It is trying to redefine undetected losses, identified under the euphemisms of pilfering, shoplifting and fiddling, as crime and is doing so in ways that can be generally appreciated and vigorously upheld. Presenting 'employee perks as the thin end of the wedge' and getting management theory to work for the security officer (Gadwall, 1975:348) are part of the approach. Favouring a firm policy on reporting and prosecution is another. Thus it is argued that 'a weak employer is never respected and minor perks and fiddles can grow alarmingly to considerable lost profits' (Saunders, 1974:259).

Beyond this there are those who feel that time has come for enforcing security by legislation as a management responsibility (Hamilton, 1974:94). As the editorial of *Security Gazette* has posed it, 'Imagine that by the year 2000, say, the maintenance of certain standards of security in premises of all kinds will have become mandatory, compliance with the law being enforced by a Security Inspectorate, comparable with the present H.M. Inspectorate of Factories . . .' (*Security Gazette*, 1974b:441). When we imagine that not-so-fanciful projection, we can see clearly how the treatment of hidden-economy activity as theft is largely in the interests of the ever-growing commercial security companies. More importantly, we can begin to appreciate the problems posed by the private security organisation as a method of controlling the hidden economy.

PROBLEMS WITH PRIVATE SECURITY

There are two fundamental problems associated with the emergent private security solution as a method of controlling the hidden economy. The first concerns the political implications of commercial policing; the second, the effectiveness of private security as a method of control.

Political problems

As some commentators have recently argued (Bowden, 1977; Bunyan, 1976), a crucial problem arises when private security moves from protection, such as the escorting of cash in transit, the supervision of wage packets, the patrol of factories, the provision of burglar alarms and so on, to making employee-status inquiries and providing plain-clothes detectives. Tom Bowden has shown that the private police force expanded and then consolidated their activities in areas yielded by the civil police, before moving on to a wider policing base that involved much more than simple protection and factory security. 'They began to get deeply involved, for example, in the very dubious area of testing the loyalty and honesty of employees and potential employees' (Bowden, 1977:349). He shows how in 1973, for example, a firm called Complete Security Service Ltd., then a subsidiary of Securicor, sent out a circular offering employers 'a man planted among your employees to report on untoward behaviour and to undertake research into the background and antecedents of workers' (Bowden, 1977:351). Nor is this approach a recent, unplanned development. There is evidence that such activity has been behind the private security approach since it was first founded. Thus in an American Management Association publication of 1950 the following 'preventative programme' was recommended to combat employee theft:

142

The only way this can be handled, I think, is by creating a department of the firm similar to the Inspector General's Department in the Army. Such a department should have an independent office in no way connected with the firm at all and to be known only to, say, the president of the firm ... These men should make general inspection tours of the homes and in an undercover method observe the habits of all the employees that handle funds ... But this problem has to be handled absolutely independently. These investigators cannot be known to any employee of the firm. They must never come to the companies' offices—they must never be seen. (McDonald, 1950:16)

More recently the U.N. Committee on Crime Prevention and Control stated that, in addition to its major task of providing guard services, a function of the industry was to provide certain investigation services. These, the Committee said, 'might include background inquiries regarding potential employees of private companies—inter alia, investigations relating to alleged misconduct on the part of company employees and investigations to determine an individual's credit rating or character' (Stead, 1975:381).

However, the political background and ethos of private security companies is supportive of business and of free enterprise. This is not surprising for, as Bowden says, 'no matter how much the private police profess to "care" for their customers, they are in existence to make profits themselves as well as guard, maintain, and help maximise the profits of others' (Bowden, 1977:351). Securicor's wider aims, for example, include the belief that 'business cannot be divorced from living; both should be nobly done'.

The political danger of this position, particularly for the Left, is that not only hidden-economy activity but also strikes and other collective activities of organised labour will come to be seen in terms of loss. As Bowden points out, 'the striker, the industrial spy and the radical trade-union activist on the shop floor are natural enemies, for, by stopping production, they are in effect putting at risk the profits that commercialised private policing is dedicated to protect' (Bowden, 1977:351).

143

Tony Bunyan has argued that this kind of approach has already led to the gathering of information on the political activities and affiliations of workers and labour movement groups. He also says some of the umbrella organisations, such as the Economic League and the British United Industrialists, also issue propaganda against 'strikes' and in favour of 'free enterprise' (Bunyan, 1977). When these political positions are supported by private security forces, it becomes difficult to deny the charge that they are private armies of the Right and that we are one step away from fascism and the *Frei Korps*. The fact that the private security companies' total manpower is well over 100,000 and that in 1975 Securicor, one of the big four companies, had 300 branches, 18,000 staff, 3,000 armoured vehicles, over 1,000 ferocious guard dogs, a network of shortwave radio masts and thirty-five specially constructed security depots adds a chilling degree of plausibility to this argument.

Ultimately, of course, the question of controlling the hidden economy through the use of private security companies focuses on the control issue. In short, how do we control the controllers? The basic difficulty here stems from the fact that, unlike the situation in the U.S.A., Canada and most of western Europe, Britain's private security industry is unrestrained other than by conventions and laws that apply to the private citizen. Indeed, the whole basis of British private security is founded on the citizen's right to arrest. In Germany, France, Canada, the U.S.A. and Switzerland a body of law has been designed to protect the privacy of the individual from commercialised investigation agencies; the companies are registered and licensed and therefore controlled to a degree not observed in Britain. In the area of the control of private security, the United Nations has expressed general agreement that where private security firms are in operation there should be regulations. These might take the form of licensing, screening and the requirement of basic qualifications by a public authority. It recorded that 'private security organisations should be subjected to a measure of public control' (Stead, 1975:38).

It has often been suggested as an alternative argument that the private security industry should best control itself through the British Security Industry Association, on the grounds that 'the best form of discipline is self-discipline' (Smith, 1975:383). It has been argued by the assistant editor of *Security Gazette*, K. G. Wright (1975), that a working party should be set up by the Home Office to include B.S.I.A. representatives but containing mainly customers of the security industry and those who work with it. The working party, says Wright, should be given three months in which to produce a detailed code of practice for the security industry, and security firms should be licensed to conform with this code. A supervisory council should be set up to maintain the code and should be given powers to revoke licences where its provisions were persistently ignored or set aside.

But the crucial question here is: if self-regulation is the best form of control for the private security industry, why is it not the best form of control for the hidden economy? Indeed, if such a principle is justifiable for that industry, it makes the industry itself redundant. This argument will be the focus of the final chapter.

Effectiveness of private security

At a conference on major property crime held at Edinburgh University in 1975, the question was raised of whether the cost of crime was high enough to justify the expenditure of so much money and effort on crime prevention. More precisely, it was argued that there is little or no evidence to show that security is really cost-effective. A year earlier, Carter (1974) had argued that about half of the total cost of crime (which he estimated at 2 per cent of the national income) was the cost of loss prevention, prosecution and punishment. Carter argued that only if loss prevention and the arrest and punishment of offenders could be provided at no cost to the community would it be worthwhile to reduce theft losses to nil. In practice, he said, the community has to decide how much theft it can afford to prevent.

Clearly, a crucial dilemma for the economic or cost-effective analysis of controlling hidden-economy activity is what is taken to be 'loss'. If all activities which detracted from profits were

145

taken as 'loss', then employees would be expected to work for nothing. Fortunately, this is not how wage-earning is seen by most companies. Wages and salaries are taken into account as part of the economic 'costs' of production. The problem occurs with activities such as pilfering, fiddling and trading. These are considered by *some* employers as part of the costs of production. But employers are increasingly being urged to see these costs as unnecessary *losses* and that further costs (of security and crime prevention) are necessary in order to cut these losses. Thus, in retail business, for example, the Group 4 Total Security Company claim that a retailer who spends £1 on their services should save at least £2 on his losses in staff theft and customer shoplifting. As a rule of thumb, the company says, shopkeepers should be prepared to devote 0.1 per cent to 0.5 per cent of their turnover to security (Goodman, 1976:13). In London's Oxford Street shops are spending around £5m per year on security to combat an estimated £10m worth of losses. This is without the additional cost of £20 for each case that is brought to court. (In 1975 31,000 cases of theft by shop staff were reported to the police (Goodman, 1976:13).)

In industry, there is the additional cost of worker resistance. If workers see increases in security and policing eroding their social benefits, resistance may take a number of economically costly forms, depending upon factors such as the degree of collectivisation of the work force, the nature of its technology and the state of its industrial relations. Resistance can range from an increase in labour turnover, to go-slows, work-to-rules, overtime bans or outright strikes, and it can involve issues quite removed from those to do with pilfering, fiddling and dealing and their control. A good example of this was the recent case of British Rail buffet-car stewards, who worked to rule on the introduction of a new fiddle-proof system for serving tea and coffee. Rather than admit that they would lose their fiddle—traditionally carried on by using their own coffee to make up drinks—the stewards claimed that the public were being denied their right to a 'decent cuppa' and that passengers were being sold an inferior product (*New Society*, 1976:163).

Of course, it will always be argued, especially by private

146

security companies, that without controls the situation would be much worse. This is much like the argument for taking vitamin tablets to prevent colds. People may argue that the tablets do not work because they still get colds. Vitamin tablet manufacturers, on the other hand, argue that a person might have caught many more colds if he had not taken the tablets. The argument is unprovable. However, I contend that in the case of hidden-economy controls, expenditure on security actually represents an economic *loss*. The assumption made, notably by security companies, is that pilfering, fiddling and dealing start suddenly at the instigation of either the odd, morally defective individual who is unable to resist temptation, or of the criminally dishonest person who has planned to steal. It is argued that these 'bad apples' will affect the rest of the work force if they are not stopped in their prime. Furthermore, it is felt that by not taking security precautions, managements encourage employee theft. Thus, Robert Traini has argued:

> Employees who find they are in a position to supplement their earnings by means of fiddles may be—indeed, often are—corrupted when they would otherwise remain honest servants. New employees are suborned into becoming part of the long-standing conspiracy. And where these fiddles become an accepted part of the job, it is easy for a situation to arise where the swindle money is taken for granted as a 'tax free perk'—and any attempt to interfere with the practice may then be regarded as equivalent to a wage cut and be resisted very strongly—even to the point of going on strike. (Traini, 1973:456)

I take a contrasting view to this. I have tried to show throughout this book that hidden-economy activity is not something that suddenly grows. Rather it is, and always has been, a part of the *costs* of production. Like wages, it provides another set of satisfactions, in this case to do with the personalised nature of work and the relationship between labour and property ownership. I do not share the view of those who argue that fiddling and pilfering is a form of payment in kind (Ditton, 1977a). I believe that working involves an affiliation with property

147

which renders a part of that property the ownership of those working on it. It is not a material relationship with property and cannot be bought with money. In other words, hidden-economy activity is, in my view, a natural, ever-present feature of human work. The implications of this for controlling the hidden economy are considerable. By paying for security, employers are creating an additional, unnecessary loss which, in turn, may be multiplied by lost production through strikes. But there is an even more ironic consequence of the employment of external security or policing agencies. This concerns the natural control that already exists within the hidden economy. As Gerald Mars and I have argued elsewhere, by removing the responsibility for self-control from the hidden economy, the introduction of external control policies may actually exacerbate the activity (Henry and Mars, 1978). The attitude may become: 'I can do what I want because it's up to them to stop me. That's what they're here for.' In short, I believe that instead of cutting losses, the introduction of private security to control the hidden economy actually results in three-fold losses.

From the foregoing discussion it would appear that the existing ways of controlling the hidden economy are unsatisfactory. Formal, legal control, as well as stigmatising the offender, completely misrepresents his activity by imposing a material value on the transactions and by failing to understand or reconstruct the events. Employers' private justice is arbitrary, unfair and wide open to abuse, and private security is politically and economically dubious. However, there is an alternative enforcement policy which could avoid these difficulties. I shall concentrate on this in the final chapter.

8. A Policy for Crime Control

> In the long run it is the evolving social structure that shapes the human condition and, accordingly, the pattern of crime in society. The police and the criminal justice system—even when performing at a high level of effectiveness—can have only a minimal impact upon the crime problem. The increases in the crime problem since 1950 took place in spite of a substantial increase in police budget, equipment and presumably effectiveness. It's not the police and the law that prevent crime; it's the community.
>
> *Theodore Ferdinand* (1977:33)

Under the influence of various pressures and taking into account the factors that I discussed in the previous chapter, the hidden economy will undoubtedly become an increasingly important focus for crime-control policy. The publicity it has received is enough to have made the whole hidden economy a 'reported crime'. As such, it is an activity about which 'something ought to be done'. But what? As we have seen, several difficulties are likely to arise if we apply conventional external law enforcement and control policies. Unless it can be shown that the use of police or of private security agencies would be more efficient in all respects than the existing practices of commercial control, then we should think long and hard about using them. Interventionist approaches have been adopted far too readily in other aspects of our lives, often at the expense of people with problems and to the benefit of the interventionists. Social

149

workers, psychiatrists, therapists, police and probation officers are a few of the many groups of interventionist agents who have made their living from the bogus claim that they know best how to run other people's lives, solve their problems and make the world a better place to live in.

So far as the hidden economy is concerned, the questions we have to answer are: (1) is it absolutely certain that intervention is necessary and, (2) are we aware of all the possible effects? If there is any doubt about the answers to these questions we should not proceed with interventionist control. Beyond this, we may look for an alternative enforcement policy to the conventional approach.

Conventional control philosophy rests on two conflicting assumptions that underlie our contradictory thinking about honesty and dishonesty. The first is that any kind of crime, if left unchecked, will naturally escalate. This 'thin edge of the wedge' argument is based very largely on a fear of what might happen, rather than on sound understanding of what does happen. The second assumption is that real crimes are committed by other people, not by oneself. Taken together, these assumptions lead to the contradictory position in which particular people or groups feel they are capable of controlling their own behaviour but that 'society' ought to do something about other people's crimes. For this reason, the private security industry argues that its own crimes do not need external controls: 'the best form of discipline is self-discipline.' The same view is held by the civil police, who believe that they are the people best fitted to investigate and discipline their officers' 'indiscretions'.

As has already been stated, I share the view that self-regulation is the best form of control. However, I believe that such an attitude renders many current police and court functions redundant. Just as the crimes of police are best controlled by the police, so the crimes of ordinary people are best controlled by themselves. I maintain, therefore, that the most appropriate solution to the issue of controlling the hidden economy is one based upon the spontaneously evolved, normative controls found to operate among participants in the hidden economy.

150

NATURAL NORMATIVE CONTROL

Normative control of crime, by which I mean group or community control, is not a new phenomenon. If we look, for example, at how untoward behaviour was controlled in early colonial America, we can see that the family, community and church maintained a firm grip on all of their members. Theodore Ferdinand (1977) in his excellent review of the American criminal justice system, says that the few newcomers who were not members of established groups, such as a family or the church, were required to join within a reasonable period or leave the community altogether. 'There was no room, particularly in New England, for independent individuals, and those who would not submit to close community control over their lives were not welcome' (Ferdinand, 1977:2). He describes how many New England communities instituted town meetings where local matters could be considered, solutions proposed and a policy established by voice-vote of those attending. Few individuals felt strong enough to defy the consensus of the town meeting and those that did were often obliged to depart as a result of public pressure.

Ferdinand points out that this form of control, by well defined permanent groups, ensured social conformity in the community, and it worked well. There was little crime and most offenders were dealt with by informal proceedings. The law was little more than an extension of the community and its mores. 'Community sentiment was more powerful in determining who was to be arrested than the written law' (Ferdinand, 1977:3). The law and its interpretation in the courts was left largely to community leaders rather than to trained lawyers or judges. Magistrates and Justices of the Peace often created law to fit cases that came before them and trials by jury were rare. When a case did reach a jury, says Ferdinand, the jury 'often formulated law, weighed evidence, and rendered verdicts more in terms of local custom than legal precedent' (Ferdinand, 1977:4). He summarises the position as follows:

Thus the court and its officers were tied to the local community in a hundred ways and followed closely the initiatives and

guidelines established by community leaders. The principal bul-
warks against deviancy and crime, therefore, were the community and the church, with the formal law and the courts
simply reinforcing their authority in nearly all matters. (Ferdinand, 1977:4)

Similarly, if we look cross-culturally rather than historically,
we can find examples of extremely effective community controls
limiting the incidence of deviant behaviour and crime. A particularly illustrative example is the poppy growers of Turkey. The
poppy is known to have been grown in Asia Minor for more
than 5,000 years, but there is no appreciable use of, or addiction
to, opium among the poppy farmers. For years it was imagined
that the strict code of the Islamic religion played an important
part in preventing people from using opium, but the fact that
the problem is extensive in other Islamic countries undermines
this argument. In a recent study Alaeddin Akcasu of the University of Istanbul has shown that the inhibition about opium
use stems from 'a deep "traditional culture" which has succeeded,
through the ages, in creating the proper psychological state,
leading to an almost total abstention from opium use, except
for immediate medical reasons' (Akcasu, 1976:13). In his survey,
conducted in thirty-five villages in the five provinces where poppy
growing is a major occupation, Akcasu found that, while 85
per cent of the sample used poppy seeds, leaves and oil as
food stuffs, only 0.3 per cent used opium. He concluded that
the actual number of opium addicts among the villagers was
negligible. Akcasu explained this by showing that almost all
parents teach their children that opium is dangerous to their
lives and should not be eaten. Almost 90 per cent of opium-grow-
ing people have learned this by the age of ten (Akcasu, 1976:15).
He accounts for the limited use of opium by the community
pressure which is applied on fellow villagers who use opium.
He found that 99 per cent of villagers had negative attitudes
toward those who used opium:

One of the most important aspects of rural life is the fact
that living in a Turkish village depends largely on one's
relations with fellow villagers. ... In almost all villages the

152

use of opium for other than medical purposes was discredited. Since opium users are discredited by fellow villagers, life thus becomes unbearable for them in such surroundings and they are forced to leave for other places. This is a strong social pressure forcing people to abstain from opium use. (Akcasu, 1976:   )

We need not look to history or across cultures to find examples of spontaneous, normative control at work. At a more general level, it is gradually being realised that an alternative form of social control for a whole range of social deviance is that exercised by the deviants themselves. The vast mushrooming of self-help groups in the broad 'health' field which has occurred over the last decade is testimony to a growing awareness of this principle. Various forms of deviancy, ranging from alcoholism, gambling, smoking, obesity and anorexia to indecent exposure, child abuse and wife battering, are found to be best controlled, handled and managed not by professional interventionist agencies such as doctors, psychiatrists or social workers, but by groups of deviants themselves, groups like Alcoholics Anonymous, Gamblers Anonymous, Smokers Anonymous, Weight Watchers, Anorexic Aid, Cui Bono, Parents Anonymous, and Women's Aid (Robinson and Henry, 1977).

Nor need we rely on examples of crime outside the hidden economy. Moral control by group pressure has always existed in the context of the hidden economy. People who fiddle and pilfer from work and trade the proceeds apply their own definitions and rules to what constitutes theft, whom one should take from and what and how much one should take. For example, Donald Horning (1970), in his study of pilfering at a television manufacturing firm, found that various work groups have norms governing pilfering at the plant. While the norms do not specify what constitutes a reasonable amount of pilfering, according to Horning they

... do provide two broad guidelines for the pilferer. The first sets the limit by indicating that pilfering should be confined to the valueless property of uncertain ownership. The second indicates that pilfering should be limited to that which is

153

needed for personal use. To exceed these limits was viewed as a threat to the entire system. (Horning, 1970:62)

As one of Horning's subjects told him, 'The workers frown on people who do it on a large scale because they're afraid the company will crack down on everyone.'

Similarly, Gerald Mars, in his study of longshoremen (dockers), found that the workers placed limits on the amount of material that it was felt acceptable to take from the docks. According to Mars, an economically 'rational' limit is set, which is linked through management collusion to an accepted maximum. Dockers call this process of obtaining this entitlement 'working the value of the boat'.

Thus, if a boat is expected to provide ten hours' work at $2 an hour then the boat is 'good for' $20 in wages. 'Working the value of the boat' in this case would mean obtaining cargo up to but not more than an estimated value of $20. (Mars, 1974:224)

But, as Mars points out, if a man takes more than the value of the boat, he is taking more than his *moral* entitlement and this alters the nature of his action. Although to an outsider the difference might well appear only one of degree, to a long-shoreman the difference is essentially qualitative. 'Up to an agreed level, pilfered cargo is seen as moral entitlement; beyond this, additional pilferage is theft' (Mars, 1974:226).

In my own study of trading networks, the same limiting and self-control processes were found to operate. Thus, we saw that Stan distinguished between 'stealing', which was breaking into premises, and 'pilfering the odd box of this or that' from the place where he worked. He felt that stealing was 'bad' and 'wrong', but that pilfering 'they don't consider wrong really . . . 'it's just perks'. Similarly, Derek distinguished between 'morally illegal stealing' which was 'hawking' stuff around and making a profit, and 'technically illegal' trading in which 'nobody is actually making money'. The same taboo against selling pilfered goods for money was found by Horning (1970:61).

154

As well as these moral distinctions, I found limits placed on the amount of goods traded, and rules governing whether or not someone was being taken for granted as a supplier. Stan, for example, said that one of the reasons trade was limited to the network of family and friends was that it could become too regularised: 'Well, you've only got to start letting everyone have it and people say, "Oh, yes, fair enough", and then they want a constant supply and start "umming and ahing" if they don't get it.' In such an event the activity becomes mundane and routine and the specialness of the relationships is eroded as they change from social to economic. The choice and spontaneity involved in trading is lost, and what perhaps began as an enjoyable diversion from the routine of work becomes itself routine and laborious. When this happens trading will be cut back or even stopped. As Lucy told me:

> I didn't mind carrying it to work but it started to get too much. People were asking me for this and that and I couldn't carry all these things on ordinary journeys to work. I worried about the money and collecting it and counting it. It all got too much to cope with so I stopped it.

Moreover, it is only when the trade is on a relatively small scale that the dealer can effectively suppress a concern over the illegality of the operation. If much money is made, or large quantities of goods change hands, the activity becomes difficult to justify morally.

Of course, statements by participants distinguishing between what is right and wrong, when referring to those involved in illegal activity, cannot be taken at face value. As we have seen in Chapter Three, in certain circumstances they may also serve as rationalisations, excuses and justifications that mask any idea of immorality in a wider sense. However, no matter what functions they serve in the broader structure of events, they are, nevertheless, rules of behaviour which are adhered to in the context of the activity. Thus, when such excesses occur, social control, usually in the effective form of social ostracism, is operated by the other members of the hidden-economy network. In some cases, as Horning showed, the sanctions applied by the group may be simply negative ones: 'Those who exceeded the limits were no longer granted the tacit support of the work group, which includes the right to neutralise one's guilt feelings and deny oneself the definition of one's acts as theft' (Horning, 1970:62). But more severe measures may be taken, as Mars showed. When one docker took too much cargo, over and above the 'value of the boat', his fellow dockers broke into his car and shared the goods among themselves. In other cases, the degree of social ostracism is harsh. If an outsider tries to move in on the group's benefits or breaks the group rules, he is rejected. A recent report by Adrian Needlestone shows how this operates among stewards on English cross-channel ferries. The fiddles are controlled by a small group of seamen known as the 'Newhaven Mafia', who hold the plum jobs. None of the casually employed summer crew get their jobs: 'As Newhaven men, they feel they have a God-given right to the job and that they will see anyone else off.' One ex-steward in Newhaven claimed that he had been sacked after being 'framed' by the 'Mafia'. He had worked for a few years on the shop and was an 'associate member' of the Mafia, but he got a conscience about it: 'When I confronted some of the blokes they said that as Newhaven men they were entitled to everything they got. Well, they did me good and proper, and I'm off the ferry now' (Needlestone, 1976:6). Given this degree of group control and the norms limiting the size and amount of goods that can be taken, it is less surprising that Derek should comment, 'It doesn't seem to multiply at all' and 'It doesn't get any worse or any more rampant.'

However, all these are spontaneous control systems which have emerged to satisfy the needs of particular situations. More recently there have been deliberate, planned attempts to establish deviancy controls based on group norms and sanctions.

PLANNED USE OF NORMATIVE REGULATION

There is a number of situations in which, despite the existence of formal control techniques, groups have been given the responsibility for controlling their members' deviance. For example, in the 1977 Notting Hill Carnival, a kind of 'self-policing' was used. The 1976 Carnival had seen riots between West Indians and police, and to avoid this in 1977, a number of the Carnival's organisers from the local Notting Hill community were used as 'stewards' while the police kept a 'low profile'. The operation was a partial success, with local stewards managing 'to defuse a potentially dangerous crowd and send them home, all without too much trouble or any police intervention' (Mackie, 1977:11). Although police were eventually used to break up gangs that formed, it is difficult to know whether they would have formed had the police not been waiting in the wings with riot shields and truncheons, inviting provocation.

Another example of the planned use of group control in place of formal intervention by outside agencies is that of the English pornography publishers. In the aftermath of a total failure of conventional police efforts to enforce the law on pornography, and the eventual protection racket which allowed it to continue, the pornography publishers decided to form their own association. This was intended to place strict controls on individual members to keep their publications within legal limits. Any member who failed to conform was to be expelled from the association.

A similar example of group control is to be found in British wage-control policy. The failure of wage-policy legislation and its legal enforcement under the Industrial Relations Act, and the defeat of the Conservative Government in 1973, led to the informal control of wage demands under the 'social contract'. British trade unions agreed to limit their own members' wage demands in exchange for certain social concessions. This form of self-control worked well for the duration of the 'contract' and enabled wage inflation in Britain to be cut from 30 per cent to 8 per cent over two years.

All these examples of the planned use of group normative sanctions to control member deviance are, in a sense, *ad hoc* developments, designed to suit particular situations as existing controls broke down. However, a significant development in the planned use of self-regulation has emerged from the work of Lawrence Kohlberg, a Harvard University professor of psy-

157

chology. Kohlberg's research, carried out over the past twenty-five years, is based on a study of moral development in children. Kohlberg (1968; Kohlberg and Kramer, 1969) hypothesises six stages of moral development, each in succession involving a more adequate, more comprehensive way of solving moral problems than those of the earlier stages. At stage one, the law is used as a force of the powerful to obtain obedience through punishment of the weaker party. In stage two, law is interpreted by expediency; one aims to satisfy one's own needs. At stage three, people obey the law because others expect they should; and at stage four, the emphasis is on fixed definitions of the law as being necessary to stop the decay of society. Stage five is that at which legal contracts are emphasised and at which law is an agreement among social equals, with defined duties for the state and the individual. The most significant stage in Kohlberg's theory is stage six, in which, he argues, there is a rational basis for ethical decisions. At this stage, the law is subordinate to justice where law and justice conflict. The unsatisfactory part of Kohlberg's theory is its evolutionary theme. Indeed, to suggest that the rational basis for ethical decisions is the last stage, and that law as a force of the powerful is the first, is somewhat naive. As Ferdinand has shown, in American colonial society such community control operated until various changes removed the administration of criminal justice from the control of local groups 'in favour of a bureaucratic élite who formulated criminal justice policy much more narrowly in terms of criteria often far removed from the moral temper of the people they were serving' (Ferdinand, 1977:8).

Kohlberg's theory has been applied in schools in a series of moral discussion classes. But as Peter Scharf (1977), one of Kohlberg's co-workers, has reported, 'if the moral education programme was to be effective it needed to create a moral community which treated members with both respect and fairness' (Scharf, 1977:104). Scharf reports that the first attempt to create a 'just community' programme began in a Connecticut female prison in 1971. Until then, hostility between inmates and guards had almost caused a riot. During 1971 inmates, guards and administrators met in a 'constitutional convention' and rules were proposed for a model democratic framework in which 'inmates would control internal discipline and define objectives and activities. All prison offences, apart from the major felonies, would be referred to a "cottage community meeting"' (Scharf, 1977:104). The community works as follows. A community member can call a meeting at any time and when a 'cottage rule offence' is discovered, the meeting acts as jury to determine guilt or innocence. If discipline is called for, it is referred to a discipline board which, says Scharf, 'includes two inmates and one staff member, chosen at random':

> Routine issues, involving matters like work assignments, love triangles or personal conflict, are dealt with through open discussion. The community occasionally deals with issues of contraband, assault and attempted escape. Cottage rules are redefined every twelve weeks in a marathon meeting. Here, there are often further negotiations with administrators as to the kinds of issues that cottage democracy may deal with. (Scharf, 1977:104)

Like the self-help groups that operate in the health field (Robinson and Henry, 1977), there is an immense difference between the 'just community' and conventional psychotherapy. Inmates at the institution are not 'diagnosed' or 'treated'. There are no assumptions that inmates are more sick, more anti-social or more neurotic than anyone else. In addition, the absence of professionals, says Scharf, 'makes it more difficult for programme staff members to exempt themselves from the judgements of the group or to deny the moral claims of inmates by means of psychotic roles, labels or terminology' (Scharf, 1977:105).

In the six years that the system has operated, it has been a phenomenal success. There have, according to Scharf, been only three escapes, and almost no acts of serious violence. Return rates to prison are roughly half the normal numbers for groups matched for age, race and crime. The success of the prison groups has encouraged Kohlberg and Scharf to begin similar projects with groups of high-school students. In these, as in the prison, the students create the school rules and curriculum aims as well as carrying them out and enforcing them.

159

In Scotland a similar form of the 'just community' has been developed in an experiment at the special unit of Barlinnie Prison in Glasgow. As in America, the unit was started after a breakdown of the conventional control system. In 1972 isolation cells or 'tiger cages' were introduced and resulted in a bloody riot. Four prisoners were accused of trying to murder six warders; one of the warders lost his eye; others were stabbed. But in 1973, on the recommendation of a Scottish Home and Health Department report, a special unit was established. The unit, as in the Connecticut system, is run communally:

> Internal matters are decided on at a weekly meeting attended by prisoners and staff, each with one vote. Discipline is dealt with by the community. A startling sense of comradeship evolved in the unit. Instead of the 'them' and 'us' attitude between prisoners and warders, 'them' and 'us' came to denote the unit and the rest of the prison system. (Hilton, 1977:12)

Following the unit's introduction, there have been no assaults on the staff. One prisoner, for example, who was sentenced for murder in 1967 and in the following five years attacked the prison system, changed dramatically. Since his involvement in the special unit, he has held an exhibition of sculpture at the Edinburgh Festival and has written a book of his experiences in the unit: *A Sense of Freedom* (Boyle, 1977).

However, it is one thing to show how the community control system works within the confines of a prison system. But would Kohlberg's theory work as well outside this system? In particular, could it be applied to the control of the hidden economy?

A SYSTEM OF COMMUNITY CONTROL

In a paper written with Gerald Mars I have briefly outlined a system in which the same kind of controls that operate in the 'just community' and self-help groups could be exercised by setting up of some form of court, situated in the work

160

place and composed of elected workers and management (Henry and Mars, 1978). Such a system is not without precedent, however. For some time it has been recognised that in the retail industry the best crime prevention methods do not come under the heading of security: 'A well trained staff not only keeps an eye on merchandise, but creates goodwill for the shop' (Goodman, 1976:13). But it is not simply a matter of crime prevention training. It is crucial that there should be involvement of staff in the decision-making process. In some American stores, for example, it has been acknowledged that the most powerful influence on an individual's behaviour are the norms of behaviour of the employee group. David Wainwright reports that a supermarket chain in New York State 'used the idea of norms as a non-threatening way of asking for help on controlling shrink in one of their markets' (Wainwright, 1976:18). He says that store employees felt much more comfortable about discussing group behaviour than individual attitudes and responsibility. They produced an action plan and then organised price checks and a rota to watch for shoplifting. Wainwright reports a manager in the supermarket chain saying that, 'once the employee group was involved, several individuals helped him with action to discourage employee theft although at no time did the employees plan action on employee theft. The employee committee seemed to accept the management norm that "around here you don't talk about employee theft"' (Wainwright, 1976:18). Wainwright reports that the success of the system using employee norms as a control was outstanding. The supermarket cut its losses in the year by two-thirds, from the dollar equivalent of £24,000 to just under £8,000.

In England the most sophisticated system of community control of the hidden economy is that operated at the Cadbury Schweppes factory in Birmingham. The system, run in conjunction with the unions on site, is officially known as a 'joint disciplinary tribunal'. Stuart Cheshire, who is a District Secretary of the Birmingham Transport and General Workers' Union (T.G.W.U.), and who has worked at the factory for eighteen years, told me how the tribunal works. The scheme, which has existed in the company for many years, consists of a tribunal composed of management, and trade-union lay officials. The tribunal procedure is initiated by the personnel department, following reports from the investigation department or production departments, depending on the type of offence. There is normally an informal meeting, involving representatives from line management and the trade union, to examine the circumstances of the complaint. There it is decided whether to proceed with an informal settlement or to call together the full disciplinary tribunal in a formal meeting.

If the informal procedure is adopted, it generally means that the offence is a minor one and it is dealt with in the personnel office with the minimum representation from both management and trade union. It is important to realise that the person accused can still exercise the right to refuse the informal procedure and opt for the full tribunal.

The full tribunal will include the factory director, normally in the chair, the personnel manager as secretary to the tribunal, and representatives of both line management and the trade union. The person lodging the complaint will formally outline its nature, giving an opportunity for the tribunal and the accused (or his representative) to question the accuracy of the allegations. The person accused, or his representative, will have the opportunity to speak and once more the members of the tribunal will have the opportunity to question.

At the end of the hearing any disciplinary measure short of dismissal is jointly agreed. Should the offence be so serious as to warrant dismissal, the matter is referred to management. As Stuart Cheshire emphasises, the union representatives are, therefore, never involved in dismissing anyone. There is, he says, a final appeal avenue open to the accused, which leads to the works director and involves an outside union official, should the person want this. Stuart Cheshire stresses that the whole 'procedure does not in any way interfere with the individual's right to pursue a dismissal through the existing legal channels'. Whilst the system was designed 'primarily to deal with cases of pilfering, it has been extended over the years to deal with a number of other disciplinary matters such as smoking offences, clocking offences and work booking offences'.

However, the most advanced development of planned community control as a system of administering justice occurs as the 'community court'.

Community Courts

A community court is defined as 'a lay body dealing with a population that has objective features in common, with jurisdiction over offences otherwise criminal and with the power to impose meaningful sanctions' In this context community is taken to mean 'a group of people living or working in the same locality, supporting common goals and subject to the same laws or regulations' (Fisher, 1975:1253). Under a community court, offenders are brought before their colleagues who hear the evidence, pronounce a verdict and pass sentence. The system closely resembles closely resembles the medieval form of jury trial in which only the offender's equals could judge him. It relies on strong moral pressure being brought to bear on the offender and much use is made of his sense of shame in the eyes of those who know him.

The planned, democratic use of community courts as an alternative system for administering criminal justice has been developed and applied most systematically in socialist countries. The system has been called 'comrades' courts' in the Soviet Union, 'people's courts' in the Republic of China, 'popular tribunals' in Cuba, 'social courts' in Hungary, 'disputes commissions' in the German Democratic Republic and 'workers' courts' in Poland.

The origin of the socialist use of community courts is generally put around 1919, with Lenin's philosophy that workers should participate in the management of all state and communal affairs including the administration of justice. Since the communist revolution in China, for example, a two-tier system for the administration of justice has been introduced. One tier deals with crimes considered to be against the state, those of 'enemies of the people', and the other handles disputes among people. As Mao Tse-Tung suggested, disputes and crimes among people should be resolved by a democratic process, involving criticism, self-criticism, self-education and social and political rehabilitation (Mao, 1966). In effect, this means that most disputes are resolved through struggle sessions, poster debates and neigh-

163

bourhood or community courts. In the courts, ordinary people chosen from the workers, peasants and soldiers serve as judges and conduct 'friendly negotiations' to bring about the settlement of disputes. Indeed, the formal legal structure, with its courts and judges, is the smallest component of the Chinese legal system. According to Martin Garbus, who has recently made a study of the Chinese system which he calls 'Justice without Courts', 95 per cent of all disputes are resolved without the use of the court structure, and he points out that the Chinese have an ancient adage: 'It is better to enter a tiger's mouth than a court of law' (Garbus, 1977:398).

A judge of the formal High Shanghai Court, whom Garbus interviewed, told him that in most cases the courts do not get involved but 'the neighbourhood, political or production unit where the man lives will try to resolve the dispute'. Whether a case like pilfering or fiddling from work is handled by the formal system depends, as in the West, on the value of the property involved. When the system is invoked, a judge of the People's Court, along with two factory workers selected from the factory where the crime occurred, are assigned to the case. The judge and the two workers meet with the factory workers and the defendant. They then hold a factory meeting to discuss the case and to obtain the opinions of the defendant's co-workers concerning how the case should be dealt with, whether the workers feel he is guilty and what they feel the punishment should be. As the judge told Garbus, when discussing a particular case of embezzlement of 1200 yuan (£200) from a heavy machinery factory:

After the defendant's entire political background was discussed, there was a dispute among his co-workers ... The majority felt the defendant did commit the crime, but that since he had confessed, repented and given the money back, he should be given a lenient treatment. A strong minority felt ... because the amount of money was so large and because he stole it from his own co-workers, he should be sent to prison. The judges and the workers' representatives then held a joint discussion. There was a meeting with the party committee ... [who] ... were advised that the bulk of the workers

164

felt the defendant should be leniently treated. .... Ultimately, a consensus was reached to give the embezzler a three year sentence under the surveillance of the masses. This meant he could work in the factory without any loss or privileges, but would meet with members of the factory on a regular basis so that he could be re-educated through his labour. (Garbus, 1977:400)

In this case, as in others that go as far as the formal court, the day *after* the judgment was decided the trial took place. This was an open trial in the factory which lasted two hours. After the trial, workers at the factory were selected to supervise the defendant.

Whereas the Chinese system of community participation in the administration of criminal justice has been in operation for some considerable time, in most socialist countries community courts did not flourish until their reintroduction between 1959 and 1962. A good illustration of how the east European courts work can be obtained by looking at 'comrades' courts' of the U.S.S.R.

The Soviet comrades' courts are established at factories, institutions and organisations, schools, collective farms, apartments, rural settlements and barracks. Their members are elected by secret ballot for periods of two years by a general meeting of the collective. The courts deal with a range of offences that include breaches of discipline at work, civil cases in which the amount does not exceed fifty roubles, non-serious criminal offences such as embezzlement, theft of state or social property and, according to the Soviet penal code, all minor infractions where it is evident that the offender can be rehabilitated by means of applying social pressure rather than punishment.

Comrades' courts are entitled to impose various sanctions, such as the obligation on the part of the offender to apologise to the victim; a reprimand; a warning without publicity; a fine; and a 'proposal to the administration of the enterprise or institution to transfer the offender to unskilled manual labour for a term not exceeding fifteen days' (Lapenna, 1968:100). Although they are independent of the more formal peoples' courts, their elected members are encouraged to attend regional

165

Councils of Comrades' Courts at which are present the best qualified members of comrades' courts and the lawyers and workers of judicial and procuratorial organs (Ramundo, 1965: 710).

The philosophy behind the comrades' courts is that offences are not merely the fault of an individual, but of the whole collective, who must take responsibility for them. Their purpose is 'to treat minor crimes as moral offences rather than to treat moral offences as crimes, and thereby to prevent moral offenders becoming criminals' (Berman and Spindler, 1963:844). The courts have a two-fold aim: to educate the public to the rules of the socialist society by arousing public interest in social order through mass participation; and to act as a vehicle through which the individual offender is re-educated and returned to society as a useful member (Rogovin, 1961:305). Thus, in the comrades' court, the community is the mentor and the individual the student. The socialist vision is that as a result of comradely censure and criticism, a new social morality will develop, become instinctive and cause crime to decline or disappear (Ramundo, 1965:699).

An important insight of the comrades' courts is that only those people who are the offenders' immediate community members can know his specific situation, conditions of life, relationships, and similar facts which, it is argued, have a significant bearing upon the correct resolution of the dispute. In this sense the court is very personal and is encouraged to consider fully the mitigating circumstances of the background of the offender and the context of his offence. Indeed, Lapenna (1968) says there is evidence to suggest that in eastern European countries like Yugoslavia, where workers or tenants have more control over the management of their enterprise than the Party, the comrades' courts are successful.

Problems with Community Justice

Despite their reported achievements in handling the offences which we would call hidden-economy crimes (some reports suggest a 1% recidivism rate although, as we have seen in Chapter

166

Six, considerable hidden-economy activity exists in spite of the controls), it is not surprising that these kinds of community courts have led to a number of criticisms by Western commentators, as well as from writers in the countries where they are used. A crucially important issue is the extent to which the courts are under restrictive pressures and subject to political controls by local Party officials, and the ease with which they can be influenced through press propaganda. It has been suggested that party or union control over the community court can result in the fabrication of an issue for the purpose of educating the public. It is further argued that the function of the court is merely a means of giving the state greater penetrative power via the collective, to encroach on the sphere of the individual and inhibit any deviation which may be thought dangerously individualistic (Rogovin, 1961:306). Controls and pressures such as this tend to distort the beneficial functions of community courts. As Fisher says, 'A true community court must remain independent of any political organization and influence if it is to operate effectively as an instrument of justice ... and its procedures should be overseen by the formal courts only to the extent necessary to insure that the constitutional freedoms and protections are not infringed' (Fisher, 1975:1278, 1282).

Further questions have been raised about community courts by a special study carried out during the introduction of the workers' courts in Poland in 1961. People interviewed in the study felt that workers' courts would mean two kinds of justice—one for the population as a whole and another for workers who happened to be in factories that adopted the system. Others said that because the system did not replace formal legal proceedings, there was a possibility of a double trial; one in the workers' court and a second in the magistrate's court. Several expressed the view that the courts only examined cases of manual workers and did not look at the same offences committed by managerial or executive personnel. In other words, they felt that 'workers' courts are courts for workers' (Podgorecki, 1962:148). There were also those who expressed fears about possible victimisation, incompetence and the relative harshness of public disgrace for such minor offences. Finally, there were doubts about whether the system would actually cut down the number of offences committed.

It must be stressed that the evidence available on any of these issues is extremely limited and the area is wide open to research. However, Podgorecki's study does enable us to understand how some of these issues would be dealt with. From his interviews with offenders, he did not find it was generally the case that any particular groups or factions within factories had an influence in directing cases to the workers' court. Of the forty-eight court cases examined, 29 per cent were directed to the workers' court by the factory management, 23 per cent by the police, 37 per cent by the Public Prosecutor and 10 per cent by tribunals (Podgorecki, 1962:147). Indeed, at a broad level, my own study of self-help groups shows that members do not use their organisations to promote the deviance of their members. Despite the mythology, Alcoholics Anonymous is not a drinking club; the Paedophile Information Exchange does not actively seek out children with whom to have sexual relations, and Gamblers Anonymous does not run a syndicate. All these groups are composed of people who enjoy their deviant activity, even if, to a greater or lesser extent, it causes them problems. To resolve their problems they curtail the activity (Robinson and Henry, 1977).

Clearly, the issue of double justice depends both upon the powers and the legal standing of the system of community justice, and also on the confidence that the community has in it. If the system is treated as a clearing house for magistrates' courts, then it is unlikely to be effective. In one factory examined by Podgorecki, a case was referred for re-trial in the public court. After this, the court was held in very low regard, by comparison with those workers' courts that took full responsibility for handling offences.

The problem of the contention that workers' courts are for workers and not management is a difficult one, but it could be remedied by allowing workers as well as executives to bring cases before a joint tribunal. Moreover, to imagine that our present system of justice is any less biased is to disregard the evidence on linguistic and judicial distortion that I discussed in Chapters Six and Seven, and also to fail to consider the current bias of law enforcement (Ditton, 1976b).

168

However, there is some evidence that systems of community justice can provide considerable benefits. In the examples that I discussed earlier there were certain economic benefits. In the supermarket experiment (p. 161), direct losses were cut by two-thirds over the year and no expenditure on security was necessary (Wainwright, 1976:18). The Connecticut prison example (p. 158) showed that the psychological skills usually paid for in conventional prison therapy can easily be taught to the prison inmates, which makes the programme cheaper to run than conventional custody or treatment programmes (Scharf, 1977:105). Podgorecki similarly found evidence to indicate that, since the introduction of workers' courts into factories, 'there was some decrease in' the number of thefts. Although his evidence on this is unreliable, he does show that 74 per cent of workers in his sample felt the workers' courts were an effective weapon against small thefts in factories. He says, 'A large number of workers interviewed were of the opinion that the workers' courts had a strongly deterrent influence, through the workers' fear of being discredited in the eyes of their own colleagues' (Podgorecki, 1962:145). It is also very interesting that in cases where workers made private use of factory goods, such as when they needed a piece of wood or tin plate or wanted to make occasional use of the factory tools, trials by the workers' court did not, on the whole, meet with approval.

The most important advantage of the community justice system over the alternative formal systems of control is that of the fair administration of justice. Not only does the system seem more effective than the conventional forms of control (although much more research and experimentation is needed before this can be certain), but it is actually felt to be more just. As Stuart Cheshire told me, concerning the Cadbury Schweppes tribunals:

The benefit as we see it over the years to our members, bearing in mind the obvious temptations for petty pilfering which exist in this type of industry, has been that the union has always had the opportunity to ensure fair play and consistency and has on many occasions been able to prevent more serious incidents developing. This is against the background that the company do not prosecute offenders accused of pilfering and has therefore allowed those guilty of comparatively minor offences not to be branded as thieves and has created opportunities for them to recover from minor misdemeanours.

Clearly, the communal control system has a certain advantage in respect of justice over other systems. By co-opting colleagues onto the court, committee or tribunal, the activity of the members can be reconstructed in ways which accurately reflect the context in which the offence occurred. The acts are not automatically translated into the terms of the market economy. At the same time as doing justice to the offender's own language, the presence of representatives of employers and the law enables the offender and the public's positions to be equally represented.

Similarly, Podgorecki found that the general picture of workers' opinions in all the factories investigated was that out of 149 persons interviewed, 78 per cent were in favour of the workers' courts and only 6 per cent were against them. (In Britain, a recent Market Opinion and Research International Poll found that only 45 per cent of people surveyed thought that the law courts were doing a good job (Kellner, 1977:4). He also found agreement among 73 per cent that punishment by public disgrace was 'right, just and effective' and that all of the admittedly small sample of eleven *offenders* interviewed who had been through a workers' court considered the verdict basically just, although only one-third accepted it without reservation. Podgorecki concludes:

The experiment with workers' courts was based on the assumption that old means of mass repression are becoming obsolete, and are no longer sufficient to prevent certain forms of socially harmful behaviour; and that in such cases, the pressure of opinion of the occupational groups is more effective than legal sanctions. On the whole the inquiry confirmed these hypotheses. It was also established that the effectiveness of workers' courts depends mainly on the uniformity of public opinion in the given occupational group. (Podgorecki, 1962:149)

170

It is difficult to be certain whether a system of community control similar to that operating in eastern European states could be applied successfully in the West. Eric Fisher (1975) has already suggested that it would provide an alternative to the conventional adjudicator in the criminal context. He says that besides an emphasis on informality and the use of community members, a community court would perform an adjudicatory as well as a conciliatory function. Indeed, Conn and Hippler (1974) have argued that in any community where individuals live and work in close daily contact with each other, disputes are generally exacerbated rather than healed by the traditional formal justice. They have shown that in Alaska conciliation boards developed by the natives of an urban ghetto can strengthen the community. These examples, together with the evidence of the Cadbury Schweppes tribunals, strongly suggest that although community courts are in many ways similar to the informal courts relied upon in most socialist countries, they could be established with some degree of success in the capitalist and mixed economies of the West. However, to imagine that community courts would completely eliminate hidden economy crime, would be to neglect the evidence of the Soviet hidden economy. What I suggest is that they would contain it within certain limits.

CONCLUSION

It may be too early to predict, but it would seem that the administration of criminal justice for some types of offence may be about to complete a full circle. Beginning with community control in an underdeveloped society, we have progressed through various stages of formal, professional, bureaucratic justice as industrialisation has gathered momentum. However, recent years have witnessed a new wave of dissatisfaction with centralised, bureaucratic structures through which most aspects of our life are managed. In areas as diverse as government, industry, health and welfare, the emerging trend is towards devolution, decentralisation, democratisation and popular participation. A part of

171

this trend is the de-centralisation of criminal justice to a form of community control which was once commonplace. But the differences between the new and old community controls are enormous.

The intervening period, during which the law and the courts developed an autonomy and an emphasis on, if not an achievement of, moral justice, saw a significant improvement over the early community courts, based as they were on local prejudice and ill-founded rumour. In the past, community members viewed dishonest offenders as different from themselves: as demoniac, damaged or defective. Unfortunately, the formal criminal justice system, rather than neutralising these early biases, simply translated them: Criminals are now viewed as disturbed, depraved or deprived. In other words, if people are offended, the 'fault' is seen to lie in the offender. In the past he had something missing, from his soul, his body, his mind. More latterly, his deprivation is seen to lie in his background or culture. Thus the formal administration of justice has been increasingly used to reinforce particular people's position: 'I am honest and it is others who are dishonest.' Others have put this more dogmatically: 'The law defends the thieving rich against the thieving poor. That is what capitalism is all about—calling one sort of crime honesty and another sort of honesty crime.' (Up Against the Law Collective, 1974b:2)

However, with the unveiling of the hidden economy we can see that clear-cut divisions between right and wrong are dissolved. We discover that everyone, from dustmen to doctors and from directors to dockers, is on the fiddle. The admission that 'we are a nation of petty thieves' (*The Sun*, 1976:2) might 'not make it any more acceptable morally'. But if we are *honest* we can see that dishonesty is, to a greater or lesser extent, something we are all guilty of. That this level of awareness is only just being achieved has much to do with the way those responsible for the formal administration of justice have upheld the false divisions between honesty and dishonesty.

In the light of these insights, many commentators are rapidly reaching the conclusion that only people involved in and aware of the community can act as effective forces in crime prevention and that simply increasing police and court capacity will neither solve the problems presently plaguing criminal justice systems, nor equip these systems to cope with changing trends in crime (Danzig, 1973; Ferdinand, 1977; Fisher, 1975; Versele, 1969). It is felt that the only way out of the present situation is for criminal justice and the community to be brought closer together, so that those who judge and those who are judged are part of the same society. Public participation in the adminis-tration of justice and intervention by community representatives in both criminal court proceedings and the execution of sentences is seen as the only direct and reliable means of achieving such integration (Versele, 1969:10).

Decentralisation and popularisation would have major advan-tages over the present system. They would improve the operation of various controlling agencies such as police and courts because, by integrating the responsibility of these institutions with the community, people would be made directly responsible for their own offences. Greater use of non-specialist personnel would not only close the gap between those who administer justice and those who receive it, bringing back trust and respect for law, but would also be economically advantageous. In addition, a decentralised system of community justice might be more efficient and effective in preventing people from committing offences. Most importantly, the emerging system of community control, steeped in a sense of moral justice, might overcome the biases of the earlier approaches. By allowing *equal* represen-tation and involvement at *all* stages of the administration of law, both offender and offended are offered justice. Community justice makes no distinctions between good and bad, court and offender, honest and dishonest. Instead, it enables us genuinely to understand the perspectives of all parties to a criminal offence; to understand the context of the crime and the perspective of the offended. I believe that only with this degree of involvement and understanding can we ever hope to liberate ourselves from the hypocrisy of our attitude to 'crime', and only then will we be capable of controlling it.

References

A. Akcasu (1976), 'A Survey on the Factors Preventing Opium Use by Poppy Growing Peasants in Turkey', *Bulletin on Narcotics*, 28, pp. 13–17.

Anonymous (1832), 'The Schoolmaster's Experience in Newgate', *Frazer's Magazine*, 5, pp. 521–33; 6, pp. 285–306, 460–98.

Anonymous (1865), 'The Disposal of Stolen Goods', *Once a Week*, 12, pp. 128–32.

Anonymous (1946), 'Confessions of a Black Market Butcher', *Saturday Evening Post* (August 24), pp. 17, 101–4.

I. Anttila (1964), 'The Criminological Significance of Unregistered Criminality', *Excerpta Criminologica*, 4, pp. 411–14.

P. Aris (1976), '£1 billion that fell off a lorry', *Daily Express* (August 9), p. 1.

F. L. Attenborough (ed.) (1922), *The Laws of the Earliest English Kings*, Cambridge University Press.

J. Awdeley (1575), 'The Fraternity of Vagabonds' in G. Salgãdo (ed.), *Cony Catchers and Bawdy Baskets: An Anthology of Elizabethan Low Life*, Harmondsworth, Penguin (1972).

J. Baldwin and M. McConnville (1977), *Negotiated Justice: Pressures on Defendants to plead guilty*, London, Martin Robertson.

F. Barth (1959), *Political Leadership Among Swat Pathans*, London, Athlone Press.

H. S. Becker (1963), *Outsiders*, Glencoe, Illinois, Free Press.

J. Bellamy (1973), *Crime and Public Order in England in the Later Middle Ages*, London, Routledge and Kegan Paul.

W. A. Belson (1975), *The Public and the Police*, London, Harper Row.

H. J. Berman (1963), *Justice in the U.S.S.R.*, New York, Basic Books.

H. J. Berman and J. W. Spindler (1963), 'Soviet Comrades' Courts', *Washington Law Review*, 38, pp. 842–910.

O. E. Bigus (1972), 'The Milkman and his Customer', *Urban Life and Culture*, 1, pp. 131–65.

P. Blumstein *et al.* (1974), 'The Honouring of Accounts', *American Sociological Review*, 39, pp. 551–66.

P. Bohannon (1955), 'Some Principles of Exchange and Investment Among the Tiv', *American Anthropologist*, 57, pp. 60–70.

J. Boissevain (1974), *Friends of Friends*, Oxford, Basil Blackwell.

T. Bowden (1977), 'Who Is Guarding the Guards?', *Political Quarterly* (July), pp. 347–53.

S. Box (1971), *Deviance, Reality and Society*, London, Holt, Rinehart and Winston.

J. Boyle (1977), *A Sense of Freedom*, London, Pan Books.

T. Bunyan (1976), *The Political Police in Britain*, London, Julian Friedman.

T. Bunyan (1977), 'The Private Security Industry' (*mimeo*), London, The Outer Circle Policy Unit.

M. O. Cameron (1964), *The Booster and the Snitch*, London, Collier-Macmillan.

P. Carlen (1976), *Magistrates' Justice*, London, Martin Robertson.

R. L. Carter (1974), *Theft in The Market* (Hobart Papers No. 60), London, Institute of Economic Affairs.

D. Chapman (1968), *Sociology and the Stereotype of the Criminal*, London, Tavistock.

D. Chappell and M. Walsh (1974), 'Operational Parameters in the Stolen Property System', *Journal of Criminal Justice*, 2, pp. 113–29.

M. B. Clinard (1952), *The Black Market: A Study of White Collar Crime*, New York, Reinhart.

H. Codere (1950), *Fighting with Property*, New York, J. J. Augustin.

P. Colquhoun (1795), *A Treatise on The Police of the Metropolis*, 7th edition, London, Joseph Mawman.

P. Colquhoun (1800), *A Treatise on Commerce and Police Forces of The River Thames*, London, Joseph Mawman.

M. J. Comer (1977), *Corporate Fraud*, London, McGraw-Hill.

S. Conn and A. E. Hippler (1974), 'Conciliation and Arbitration in the Native Village and the Urban Ghetto' *Judicature*, 58, pp. 228–35.

C. R. Cooper (1936), 'Stolen Goods', *Saturday Evening Post* (January 18), pp. 16–7, 69–72.

D. Cort (1959), 'The Embezzler' *Nation* (April 18), pp. 339–42.

B. Cox, J. Shirley, M. Short (1977), *The Fall of Scotland Yard*, Harmondsworth, Penguin.

E. Crapsey (1871), 'The Nether Side of New York: Fences', *The Galaxy*, 11, pp. 494–502.

D. Cressey (1953), *Other People's Money*, Glencoe, Illinois, Free Press.

D. Cressey (1970), 'The Respectable Criminal' in J. Short (ed.), *Modern Criminals*, New York, Transaction-Aldine, pp. 105–16.

S. J. Curtis (1960), *Modern Retail Security*, Springfield, C. C. Thomas.

M. Dalton (1964), *Men Who Manage*, New York, John Wiley and Sons.

176

R. Danzig (1973), 'Toward the Creation of a Complementary Decentralised System of Criminal Justice', *Stanford Law Review*, 26, pp. 1–54.

J. Davis (1972), 'Gifts and the U.K. Economy', *Man*, 7, pp. 408–29.

J. Davis (1973), 'Forms and Norms: The Economy of Social Relations', *Man*, 8, pp. 159–76.

T. Dekker (1612), 'O Per Se O' in A. Judges (ed.), *The Elizabethan Underworld*, London, Routledge and Kegan Paul (1965), pp. 366–82.

J. Ditton (1976a), '"The Fiddler": A Sociological Analysis of Forms of Blue Collar Employee Theft among Bread Salesmen' (*Ph.D. thesis*), University of Durham.

J. Ditton (1976b), 'The Dual Morality in the Control of Fiddles' (*mimeo*), London, The Outer Circle Policy Unit.

J. Ditton (1977a), 'Computer Fraud' (*mimeo*), London, The Outer Circle Policy Unit.

J. Ditton (1977b), 'Perks, Pilferage, and the Fiddle: The Historical Structure of Invisible Wages', *Theory and Society*, 4, pp. 39–71.

J. Ditton (1977c), *Part-Time Crime: An Ethnography of Fiddling and Pilferage*, London, Macmillan.

J. Ditton (1977d), 'A Note on Commercial Social Control' (*mimeo*), London, The Outer Circle Policy Unit.

M. Dobbs (1977), 'Will a bit 'on the side' keep the Poles quiet?', *The Sunday Times* (September 25), p. 8.

T. Dudley (1828), *The Tocsin or a Review of London Police Establishments*, London.

E. Durkheim (1947), *Division of Labour in Society*, New York, Free Press.

F. Emerson (1971), 'They can get it for you better than wholesale', *New York Magazine*, 4, pp. 34–9.

K. A. D. England (1973), 'A Consideration of the Alienated Condition of Shopworkers in the Retail Trade' (*mimeo*).

K. A. D. England (1976), 'Fiddles in the Distributive Trades' (*mimeo*).

Evening Standard (1976), 'Surgical swindles' (September 16), p. 12.

H. A. Faberman and E. A. Weinstein (1970), 'Personalisation in Lower-Class Consumer Interaction', *Social Problems*, 17, pp. 449–57.

T. N. Ferdinand (1977), 'Criminal Justice in America: From Colonial Intimacy to Bureaucratic Formality' (*mimeo*), Northern Illinois University.

F. Field (1976), 'Background Note on Tax and Social Security Abuse' (*mimeo*), London, The Outer Circle Policy Unit.

R. Firth (1965), *Primitive Polynesion Economy*, 2nd edition, London, Routledge and Kegan Paul.

E. A. Fisher (1975), 'Community Courts: An Alternative to Conventional Criminal Adjudication', *American University Law Review*, 24, pp. 1253–91.

A. P. Franklin (1975), 'Internal Theft in a Retail Organisation: A Case Study' (*Ph.D. thesis*), Ohio State University.

J. Fryer (1976), 'Fiddling while the roast burns', *The Sunday Times* (July 11), p. 45.

J. Fryer (1977), 'Too much law is costing jobs', *The Sunday Times* (August 28), p. 53.

G. Gadwall (1975), 'Employee "perks"—tip of the iceberg or thin end of the wedge?', *Security Gazette* (October), pp. 348–9.

M. Garbus (1977), 'Justice without Courts: A Report on China Today', *Judicature*, 60, pp. 395–402.

B. Gilding (1971), 'The Journeymen Coopers of East London', *History Workshop Pamphlet No. 4.*

E. Goffman (1961), *Encounters*, Harmondsworth, Penguin.

E. Goffman (1971), *Relations in Public*, Harmondsworth, Penguin.

E. Goodman (1976), 'Self-service on a growing scale', *Financial Times* (November 27), p. 13.

A. Gouldner (1960), 'The Norm of Reciprocity: A Preliminary Statement', *American Sociological Review*, 25, pp. 161–78.

R. Greene (1592), 'The Second Part of Cony-Catching' in A. Judges (ed.), *The Elizabethan Underworld*, London, Routledge and Kegan Paul (1965), pp. 149–79.

The Guardian (1975), 'Village depot for stolen goods' (December 16), p. 5.

J. Hall (1952), *Theft, Law and Society*, Indianapolis, Bobbs-Merrill.

J. E. Hall Williams (1965), 'Sentencing in Transition' in T. Grygier *et al.* (eds.) *Criminology in Transition*, London, Tavistock, pp. 23-42.

P. Hamilton (1974), 'Legislating for Security', *Security Gazette* (March), pp. 94-5.

J. W. Harrington (1926), 'Swift punishment of crafty fences seen as key to war on theft', *New York Herald-Tribune* (April 11), p. 3.

S. Henry (1976), 'Stolen Goods: The Amateur Trade' (*Ph.D. thesis*), University of Kent.

S. Henry (1977), 'On The Fence', *The British Journal of Law and Society*, 4, pp. 124–33.

S. Henry and G. Mars (1978), 'Crime at Work: The Social Construction of Amateur Property Crime', *Sociology* (forthcoming).

I. Hilton (1977), 'Out of the tiger cages', *The Sunday Times* (August 7), p. 12.

Home Office (1973), *Shoplifting and Theft by Shop Staff*, London, Her Majesty's Stationery Office.

R. Hood and R. Sparks (1970), *Key Issues in Criminology*, London, Weidenfeld and Nicolson.

P. Hopkins (1977), 'VAT fraud that costs millions', *Daily Express* (September 22), p. 6.

D. M. Horning (1970), 'Blue Collar Theft: Conceptions of Property Attitudes toward Pilfering and Work Group Norms in a Modern Plant' in E. Smigel and H. L. Ross (eds.), *Crimes Against Bureaucracy*, New York, Van Nostrand Reinhold, pp. 46–64.

G. Howson (1970), *The Thief-Taker General: The rise and fall of Jonathan Wild*, London, Hutchinson.

C. Hudson (1977), 'How many bottles to remove one appendix?', *Evening Standard* (August 11), p. 17.

J. Huizinga (1938), *Homo Ludens*, London, Paladin.

A. Katsenelinboigen (1977), 'Coloured Markets in the Soviet Union', *Soviet Studies*, 29, pp. 62–85.

J. Kay (1976), 'Stop thief!', *The Sun* (August 9), p. 1.

P. Kellner (1977), 'Who runs Britain?', *The Sunday Times* (September 18), p. 4.

Kent Herald (1973), 'Youths sold goods "on the side"' (October 2), pp. 1, 8.

L. Klein (1964), *Multi-products Ltd.*, London, Her Majesty's Stationery Office.

C. B. Klockars (1972), 'The Fence Caveat Emptor, Caveat Vendor' (*mimeo*), presented to the American Society of Criminology Inter-American Conference, Caracas.

C. B. Klockars (1974), *The Professional Fence*, New York, Free Press.

L. Kohlberg (1968), 'The Child as Moral Philosopher', *Psychology Today*, 2, pp. 25–30.

L. Kohlberg and R. Kramer (1969), 'Continuities and Discontinuities in Childhood and Adult Moral Development', *Human Development*, 12, pp. 93–120.

D. A. Laird (1950), 'Psychology and the Crooked Employee', *Management Review*, 39, pp. 210–15.

I. Lapenna (1968), *Soviet Penal Policy*, London, The Bodley Head.

E. M. Lemert (1967), *Human Deviance, Social Problems and Social Control*, New Jersey, Prentice-Hall.

T. Lupton (1963), *On the Shop Floor*, London, Pergamon Press.

C. MacAndrew and R. Edgerton (1969), *Drunken Comportment*, London, Nelson.

L. Mackie (1977), 'View from the Hill', *The Guardian* (August 30), p. 11.

B. Malinowsky (1922), *Argonauts of the Western Pacific*, London, Routledge and Kegan Paul.

Mao Tse-Tung (1966), *On the Correct Handling of Contradictions Among the People*, San Francisco, Chinese Books and Periodicals.

G. Mars (1972), 'An Anthropological Study of Longshoremen and of Industrial Relations in the Port of St. John's, Newfoundland, Canada' (*Ph.D. thesis*), University of London.

179

G. Mars (1973), 'Hotel Pilferage: A Case Study on Occupational Theft' in M. Warner (ed.), *The Sociology of the Workplace*, London, Allen and Unwin pp. 200–10.

G. Mars (1974), 'Dock Pilferage' in P. Rock and M. McIntosh (eds.), *Deviance and Control*, London, Tavistock pp. 209–28.

G. Mars (1976), 'Some Functions of Institutionalised Pilferage' (*mimeo*), London, The Outer Circle Policy Unit.

G. Mars (1977), 'Some Implications of "Fiddling" at Work' in B. Kniveton (ed.), *The Social Psychologist in Industry*, Loughborough University Press.

G. Mars and P. Mitchell (1976), *Room for Reform: A Case Study on Industrial Relations in the Hotel Industry*, Bletchley, Open University Press.

G. Mars and P. Mitchell (1977), 'Catering: Low Pay, Low Unionism and Payment by the Fiddle', *Low Pay Bulletin* (August).

J. P. Martin (1962), *Offenders as Employees*, London, Macmillan.

D. Matza (1964), *Delinquency and Drift*, New York, John Wiley and Sons.

D. Matza (1969), *Becoming Deviant*, New Jersey, Prentice Hall.

D. May (1977), 'How the breadmen sneak their slice of the profits', *The Sunday Times* (April 17), p. 3.

M. F. McDonald (1950), *Case Study of a Prominent Dishonesty Loss*, New York, American Management Association.

P. McHugh (1977), 'The Code Breakers: Credit cards used as perks', *The Sun* (April 26), p. 2.

C. W. Mills (1940), 'Situated Actions and Vocabularies of Motive' in I. Horowitz, *Power, Politics and People*, Oxford University Press (1969), pp. 439–52.

P. Mitchell (1976), 'Fiddles: Trade Union Growth' (*mimeo*), London, The Outer Circle Policy Unit.

P. Moore (1975), 'Prosecution's role in curbing retail theft', *Security Gazette* (April), pp. 125–6.

P. Moore (1976), 'Exposed: The great trains robbery, by the buffet car fiddlers', *News of the World* (August 29), p. 7.

A. Needlestone (1976), 'Those ferry fiddlers are still at it', *News of the World* (September 19), p. 6.

New Society (1976), 'In the leaves' (July 22), p. 163.

Office of Fair Trading (1975), *Bargain Offer Claims: A Consultative Document*, London, Her Majesty's Stationery Office.

G. Orwell (1933), *Down and Out in Paris and London*, London, Secker and Warberg.

R. Palmer (1973), 'Pilfering—Industry's Hidden Losses', *Industrial Management* (Dec.–Jan.), pp. 20–4.

B. Park (1973), 'This airport scandal can no longer be hushed up', *Daily Mail* (August 7), p. 8.

M. Parkin (1976a), 'Fiddling with no strings', *The Guardian* (January 30), p. 13.

M. Parkin (1976), 'Fiddling is a lesson for the bosses', *The Guardian* (October 7), p. 7.

E. Partridge (1968), *Dictionary of the Underworld*, London, Routledge and Kegan Paul.

G. Pattison (1850), 'The Coopers' Strike at the West India Dock 1821', *Mariner's Mirror* (August 12).

J. Pettigrew (1977), 'Britain on the Fiddle', *Sunday Mirror* (January 30), pp. 22–3.

L. O. Pike (1873), *A History of Crime in England Vol. 1*, London, Smith and Elder.

A. Podgorecki (1962), 'Attitudes to the Workers' Courts' in V. Aubert (ed.), *Sociology of Law*, Harmondsworth, Penguin (1969), pp. 142–149.

K. Polanyi (1960), *The Great Transformation*, Boston, Beacon Press.

President's Commission on Law Enforcement and Administration of Justice (1967), *'Task Force Report: Crime and its impact. An assessment'*, Washington D.C., U.S. Government Printing Office.

A. Price (1977), 'The great British rip-off!' *Daily Mirror* (April 22), p. 26.

E. R. Quinney (1963), 'Occupational Structure and Criminal Behaviour: Prescription Violators by Retail Pharmacists', *Social Problems*, 11, pp. 179–85.

L. Radzinowicz (1964), 'The Criminal in Society', *Journal of the Royal Society of Arts*, 112, pp. 916–29.

B. A. Ramundo (1965), 'The Comrades' Court: Molder and Keeper of Socialist Morality', *George Washington Law Review*, 33, pp. 692–727.

Report of the Committee of Inquiry on Industrial Democracy (1977): Chairman Lord Bullock, Cmnd. 6706 London, 1977.

T. S. Rice (1928), 'Preface' to Prison Committee of the Association of Grand Jurors of New York County *Criminal Receivers in the United States*, New York, G. P. Putnam's Sons, pp. iii–xiii.

K. J. Richstein (1965), 'Ambulance Chasing: A Case Study of Deviation and Control within the Legal Profession', *Social Problems*, 13, pp. 3–17.

G. D. Robin (1965), 'Employees as Offenders: A Sociological Analysis of Occupational Crime' (*Ph.D. thesis*), University of Pennsylvania.

G. D. Robin (1970), 'The Corporate and Judicial Disposition of Employee Thieves' in E. Smigel and H. L. Ross (eds.), *Crimes Against Bureaucracy*, New York, Van Nostrand Reinhold, pp. 124–46.

181

D. Robinson and S. Henry (1977), *Self-Help and Health: Mutual Aid for Modern Problems*, London, Martin Robertson.

E. B. Rogovin (1961), 'Social Conformity and the Comradely Courts in the Soviet Union', *Crime and Delinquency*, 7, pp. 303–11.

T. Roselius and D. Benton (1973), 'Marketing Theory and the Fencing of Stolen Goods', *Denver Law Journal*, 50, pp. 177–205.

D. F. Roy (1953), 'Work Satisfaction and Social Rewards in Quota Achievement: An analysis of piecework incentive', *American Sociological Review*, 18, pp. 507–14.

M. D. Sahlins (1972), *Stone Age Economics*, London, Tavistock.

G. Salgãdo (ed.) (1972), *Cony-Catchers and Bawdy Baskets: An Anthology of Elizabethan Low Life*, Harmondsworth, Penguin.

R. F. Salisbury (1962), *From Stone to Steel: Economic consequences of technological change in New Guinea*, Melbourne, University Press.

C. Sandford (1977), 'Discussion Paper on Tax Evasion and Avoidance' (*mimeo*), London, The Outer Circle Policy Unit.

M. K. Saunders (1974), 'Preventing fuel frauds and fiddles', *Security Gazette* (July), pp. 258–60.

P. Scharf (1977), 'The Just Community', *New Society* (April 21), pp. 104–5.

M. Scott and S. Lyman (1970), 'Accounts, Deviance and the Social Order' in J. Douglas (ed.), *Deviance and Respectability*, New York, Basic Books, pp. 89–119.

Security Gazette (1974a), 'Theft and national prosperity' (October), p. 365.

Security Gazette (1974b), 'The human factor' (December), p. 441.

Security Gazette (1975), 'Britain's record £100 million theft loss in 1974' (November), pp. 378–9.

T. Sellin (1937), *Research Memorandum on Crime in the Depression*, New York, Social Science Research Council Bulletin 27.

L. Sherman (ed.) (1974), *Police Corruption: A Sociological Perspective*, New York, Anchor.

P. Shurmer (1972), 'The Gift Game', *New Society*, 18, pp. 1242–5.

G. Simmel (1950), 'The Metropolis and Mental Life' in K. H. Wolff (ed.), *The Sociology of George Simmel*, Glencoe, Illinois, The Free Press (1964), pp. 409–24.

E. Smith (1926), 'Crime has now evolved as big business', *New York Times* (September 5), p. 5.

P. Smith (1975), 'BSIA should be judged by realistic standards', *Security Gazette* (November), pp. 382–3.

P. J. Stead (1975), 'Regulation of security industry as an international problem: Points from a discussion at the 5th UN Congress on crime prevention', *Security Gazette* (November), pp. 381, 385.

J. Steiner, S. Hadden and L. Herkomer (1976), 'Price Tag Switching', *International Journal of Criminology and Penology*, 4, pp. 129–43.

The Sun (1976), 'We all pay' (August 9), p. 2.

A. Sykes (1960), 'Trade Union Workshop Organisation', *Human Relations*, 13, pp. 49–66.

T. Szasz (1973), *The Second Sin*, London, Routledge and Kegan Paul.

L. Taylor (1972), 'The Significance and Interpretation of Motivational Questions: The Case of Sex Offenders', *Sociology*, 6, pp. 23–9.

Theft Act (1968), Her Majesty's Stationery Office.

The Times (1963), 'The pilferers' reasons for fiddling' (October 18), p. 4.

J. J. Tobias (1972), *Crime and Industrial Society in the Nineteenth Century*, Harmondsworth, Penguin.

R. Traini (1973), 'The Swindles Within', *Security Gazette* (December), pp. 455–6.

R. Traini (1974), 'How Employee Dishonesty can Drain Business Resources', *Security Gazette* (May), pp. 189–90.

Up Against the Law Collective (1974a), 'Police Corruption', *Up Against the Law*, 2, pp. 21–35.

Up Against the Law Collective (1974b), 'Editorial', *Up Against the Law*, 4, p. 2.

A. Van Gennep (1960), *The Rites of Passage*, London, Routledge and Kegan Paul.

S-C. Versele (1969), 'Public Participation in the Administration of Criminal Justice', *International Review of Criminal Policy*, 27, pp. 9–17.

D. Wainwright (1976), 'High Street thieving', *The Guardian* (December 9), p. 18.

R. Wallis (1976), 'On the Fiddle', *Man Alive Programme*, B.B.C. Television, (April 22).

Which? (1977), 'How you rate your jobs' (September), pp. 489–93.

W. J. Whittaker (1895), *The Mirror of Justices*, London, Selden Society.

L. Wirth (1938), 'Urbanism as a way of life', *American Journal of Sociology*, 44, pp. 1–24.

K. G. Wright (1975), 'Has the BSIA Lost its Way?', *Security Gazette* (August), pp. 274–6.

L. R. Zeitlin (1971), 'Stimulus/Response: A Little Larceny can Do a Lot for Employee Moral', *Psychology Today*, 5, pp. 22, 24, 26, 64.

183

Name Index

Adam de Cuckfield; 6
Akcasu, A.; 152, 153, 175
Alcoholics Anonymous; 153, 168
American Management Associ-
ation; 142
Anonymous; 11, 22, 67, 68, 175
Anorexic Aid; 153
Anttila, I.; 1, 175
Aris, P.; 4, 175
Aristotle; 6
The Association for the Prevention of
Theft in Shops; 141
The Association of Grand Jurors of
New York County; 71
Attenborough, F. L.; 62, 175
Aubert, V.; 181
Awdeley, J.; 7, 8, 175

Baldwin, J.; 131, 175
Barth, F.; 104, 175
Becker, H. S.; 13, 175
Bellamy, J.; 7, 175
Belson, W. A.; 125, 175
Benton, D.; 23, 87, 182
Berman, H. J.; 166, 175
Bigus, O. E.; 3, 26, 113, 175
Blumstein, P.; 45, 176
Bohannon, P.; 105, 176
Boissevain, J.; 17, 176
Bowden, T.; 140, 142, 143, 176
Box, S.; vii, 2, 45, 61, 75, 176
Boyle, J.; 160, 176
British Airport Authority; 138
British Airport Police; 138
British Rail; 146
British Security Industry Associ-
ation; 140, 144, 145

British Transport Police; 138
British United Industrialists; 144
Bullock, A.; 137, 181
Bunyan, T.; 142, 144, 176
Business Barter Limited; 109

Cadbury Schweppes Limited; 161,
169, 171
Cambridge Institute of Crimino-
logy; 1
Cameron, M. O.; 2, 3, 20, 176
Carlen, P.; 121, 176
Carter, R. L.; 145, 176
Chapman, D.; 1, 2, 176
Chappell, D.; 72, 73, 176
Cheshire, S.; 161, 162, 169
Christopher, A.; 125
Clinard, M. B.; 22, 176
Codere, H.; 97, 176
Colquhoun, P.; 8, 9, 10, 63, 64, 65,
66, 69, 176
Comer, M. J.; 113, 138, 176
Complete Security Services
Limited; 142
Conn, S.; 171, 176
Conservative Government; 157
Cooper, C. R.; 71, 176
Cort, D.; 124, 176
Cox, B.; 51, 176
Crapsey, E.; 68, 69, 176
Cressey, D.; 3, 46, 176
Cui Bono; 153
Curtis, S. J.; 17, 176

Dalton, M.; 112, 132, 176
Danzig, R.; 173, 177
'Dave'; 24, 36, 38, 48, 51, 56, 88

185

Davis, J.; 100, 103, 108, 110, 111, 177
Dekker, T.; 8, 177
'Derek'; 18, 19, 24, 25, 30, 35, 36, 48, 56, 78, 81, 82, 83, 84, 85, 89, 99, 100, 101, 154, 156
'Dick'; 24, 99
Ditton, J.; 3, 5, 6, 11, 13, 26, 38, 45, 51, 53, 76, 113, 126, 129, 131, 147, 168, 177
Dobbs, M.; 116, 177
Douglas, J.; 182
Dudley, T.; 64, 66, 177
Durkheim, E.; 74, 177

The Economic League; 144
Edgerton, R.; 44, 179
Edinburgh University; 145
Edward I; 6
Edward III; 7
Elizabeth I; 7
Emerson, F.; 22, 24, 31, 113, 177
England, K. A. D.; 3, 113, 177

Faberman, H. A.; 107, 177
Ferdinand, T. N.; 149, 151, 152, 158, 173, 177
Field, F.; 2, 177
Firth, R.; 106, 177
Fisher, E. A.; 163, 167, 171, 173, 177
Franklin, A. P.; 3, 113, 178
'Freddy'; 18, 25, 26, 27, 33, 35, 81, 87, 91, 99
Fryer, J.; 4, 137, 178

Gadwall, G.; 141, 178
Gamblers Anonymous; 153, 168
Garbus, M.; 164, 165, 178
George I; 65
George IV; 62
'Gerry'; 18, 83, 85, 101
Gilding, B.; 9, 178
Goffman, E.; 40, 44, 178
Goodman, E.; 146, 161, 178
Gouldner, A.; 100, 178
Greene, R.; 8, 63, 178
Group 4 Total Security Company; 146
Grygier, T.; 178

Hadden, S.; 182
Hall, J.; 6, 7, 28, 62, 71, 72, 73, 74, 123, 127, 128, 178

Hall Williams, J. E.; 131, 178
Hamilton, P.; 141, 178
Harrington, J. W.; 70, 178
Harvard University; 157
Henry, S.; 3, 14, 20, 69, 148, 153, 159, 161, 168, 178, 182
Henry VIII; 7
Herkomer, L.; 182
Hilton, I.; 160, 178
Hippler, A. E.; 171, 176
H.M. Inspectorate of Factories; 141
Home Office; 2, 140, 141, 145, 178
Hood, R.; 131, 178
Hopkins, P.; 114, 178
Horning, D. M.; 3, 90, 113, 124, 125, 126, 153, 154, 155, 156, 179
Horowitz, I.; 180
Howson, G.; 62, 65, 82, 179
Hudson, C.; 109, 179
Huizinga, J.; 94, 96, 179

Ine; 62
Inland Revenue Staff Association; 125

James I; 7
'Jim'; 18, 25, 27, 33, 87, 97, 99
'John'; 48, 51, 82
Judges, A.; 177, 178

Katsenelinboigen, A.; 114, 115, 116, 179
Kay, J.; 4, 179
Kellner, P.; 170, 179
Klein, L.; 112, 179
Klockars, C. B.; 20, 23, 28, 44, 45, 73, 74, 86, 87, 179
Kniveton, B.; 180
Kohlberg, L.; 157, 158, 159, 179
Kramer, R.; 158, 179

Laird, D. A.; 124, 179
Lapenna, I.; 165, 166, 179
Lemert, L. M.; 13, 179
'Lucy'; 18, 24, 37, 48, 51, 57, 58, 59, 83, 87, 90, 95, 98, 155
Lupton, T.; 112, 179
Lyman, S.; 45, 46, 182

MacAndrew, C.; 44, 179
Mackie, L.; 157, 179
Malinowski, B.; 104, 179

186

Subject Index

189

Gifts; 80, 85, 91, 96, 97–8, 100, 110–11
Goods, classes of; 104, 105, 110
  conversion of; 105–6, 111
  cut price; 27
  damaged; 58
  discount; 55, 59
  free; 55, 87, 91, 96–7
  off-the-back-of-a-lorry; 4, 5, 20–3, 57, 58
  reject; 58
  stolen; 8, 19, 43, 56–8
  (see 'cheap' goods, bargains)
Guilt; 72, 79, 81, 100, 131, 156, 164, 172
  (see knowledge of illegality)

Handling stolen goods; 15, 43, 50, 121
  (see receiving stolen goods)
Harbouring 'bad men'; 62, 63, 64
'Harbouring stolen cattle'; 62
Hausa; 110
Hidden economy, attention to; 3–5, 11, 12, 111–17, 134–35
  benefits accruing to; 33
  definition of; 5–6
  discovery of; 124–25, 130
  explanation of; 11–14
  exploitation of; 132–34
  functions of; 132–34
  history of; 6–11
  reporting of; 125, 127, 136, 140, 146
  size of; 11–12, 77, 124
  study of; 5, 13–16
  toleration of; 4, 18, 30, 129, 130, 135, 145, 154
Hidden economy and legitimate jobs; 10–11, 12–13, 20, 24–5, 77–8, 90, 95–6, 127
Hidden economy as a reward; 132–34
Hidden economy in Eastern Europe; 21, 114–17
Hidden-economy trading, attractiveness of; 93, 94, 95
  context of; 18–20, 27–8, 34–5, 95–6, 97–8
  definition of; 20
  description of; 20–3
  extent of; 50, 125
  features of; 21, 33, 56, 80–102, 154–55
  history of; 61–73

income from; 20
openness of; 81
problems of; 88–9
scale of; 77, 85, 88–90, 154–56
uncertainty of; 19, 83–4
vagueness of; 19, 83–4, 85
(see trading)
Honesty; 12–13, 36–7, 39–40, 42, 49, 50, 67, 68, 69–70, 71, 72, 75–9, 90, 115, 130, 135, 142, 150, 172–73
Hustler; 22–3, 39

Incomes policy; 11, 132
Inflation; 11, 48–9, 132, 134–36
Individuality; 95–6, 132–33
Industrial democracy; 137
Injustices and inequalities; 48, 120–22, 123, 130–31, 132–33, 167
Interventionist policy; 134, 149–50, 153, 157
Interviews; 15–16, 52–3

Joint Disciplinary Tribunal; 161
Jonathan Wild; 65, 69, 81–2
Jury trials; 151–52, 163
'Just community'; 158–60
Justice; 158, 169–70
  private; 123, 124–34
  (see administration of justice)
Justifications; 10–11, 46, 49–52, 53–4, 90, 155

Kind-payments system; 84–6
Kohlberg's theory; 157–59
Knowledge of illegality; 42–3, 56–60, 65–6, 81–2, 95, 155
'Kula' exchange; 104, 110
Kwakiutl Indians; 97

Labelling theory; 13
Labelling newcomers; 34–40
Labour legislation; 137, 157
Language; 105, 106, 111, 117–22, 123
  (see talk, explanations, vocabularies)
Language of law; 45–6, 120–21
Language of market exchange; 55–60, 105, 111, 117–18, 120–22
'Larceny by servant'; 7–8, 10–11, 75, 127
Law; 42, 54, 158
Law breaking; 42–3, 124
Legal control; 120–22, 125, 131

191